MOVE IT!

WORKBOOK WITH MP3S

1

CHARLOTTE COVILL

SERIES CONSULTANT: CARA NORRIS-RAMIREZ

Contents

Starter Unit

Vocabulary • Countries and nationalities

1 Write the countries and nationalities.

Country	Nationality
¹ Spain	*Spanish*
²	English
France	³
Mexico	⁴
Greece	⁵
⁶	Brazilian

• Numbers

2 Put the numbers in order. Write them below.

eighteen	6	two hundred ninety-three
74	1,532	thirty-five

1 6 .... *six*
2 ....
3 ....
4 ....
5 ....
6 ....

• Spelling

3 Listen and write the words.
2
1 My name's *Kylie*.
2 I'm .... years old.
3 I'm from ....
4 We're at the .... Club Resort.
5 It's in ....

• Classroom objects

4 Complete the crossword.

Across

Down

• Days of the week and months of the year

5 Reorder the letters to make days of the week. Then write the days in the correct order.

1 aSudyn   *Sunday*   *Sunday*
2 Tesyuda   ....
3 adFiry   ....
4 yuTsrhda   ....
5 yWaeddsne   ....
6 traaudyS   ....
7 yadnoM   ....

6 Number the months in order.

February	☐	April	☐
June	☐	December	☐
November	☐	March	☐
October	☐	September	☐
July	☐	May	☐
January	☐1	August	☐

• Classroom language

7 Choose the one that doesn't belong.

1 November (Portugal) January February
2 book notebook May dictionary
3 Tuesday Spanish Greek Italian
4 pencil ruler eraser fifteen
5 interactive whiteboard fifteen forty one hundred
6 England France Italy Brazilian

8 Complete the conversations with these phrases.

> Can you repeat that, please?
> How do you say "mesa" in English?
> How do you spell 30?
> Open your books!
> ~~Please be quiet!~~
> What's the homework?

Grammar • To be

1 Complete the text with *'m, is/isn't, are/aren't*.

My name ¹ *is* Natalia. I ² .... twelve years old. I ³ .... from Colombia. This ⁴ .... Marco. He ⁵ .... Colombian. He ⁶ .... Italian. We ⁷ .... friends. We ⁸ .... in Italy or Colombia. We ⁹ .... in the United States on vacation.

2 Choose the correct options.

1 *I* / *You* 'm Australian.
2 *They* / *He* isn't at the park.
3 *We* / *She* are from Brazil.
4 *It* / *I* 's very tall.
5 *He* / *You* aren't fourteen.
6 *They* / *I* 'm not from London.

3 Look at the sentences in Exercise 2. Write opposite sentences.

1 *I'm not Australian.*
2 ....
3 ....
4 ....
5 ....
6 ....

4 Read the Visitors' Book. Write questions and answers about the nationalities.

• Visitors' Book •	
Name	**Country**
Bruce	England
Lucille	France
Luisa	Portugal
Nick and Theo	Greece
Javier	Spain
Rosa	Mexico
Mercedes	Mexico

1 Bruce / The US
  Is Bruce American?
  No, he isn't. He's English.
2 Lucille / France
  ....
  ....
3 Luisa / Brazil
  ....
  ....
4 Nick and Theo / Italy
  ....
  ....
5 Javier / Spain
  ....
  ....
6 Rosa and Mercedes / Mexico
  ....
  ....

- ## Wh questions

5 **Write and answer the questions.**

1 Why / here? / you / are
   Why are you here?

   I'm here because this is my school.

2 favorite / is / teacher? / Who / your

   ....

   ....

3 animal? / is / What / favorite / your

   ....

   ....

4 is / house? / your / Where

   ....

   ....

5 your / is / birthday? / When

   ....

   ....

6 old / How / you? / are

   ....

   ....

- ## This/That/These/Those

6 **Complete the sentences with *This, That, These* or *Those*.**

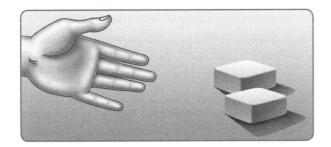

1 *These* are erasers.

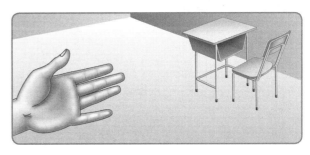

4 .... is a desk and a chair.

2 .... is a calculator.

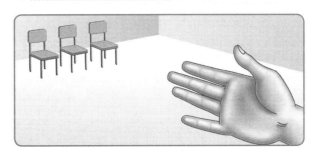

5 .... are chairs.

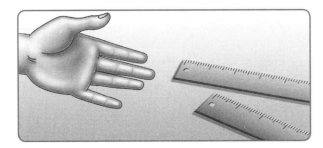

3 .... are rulers.

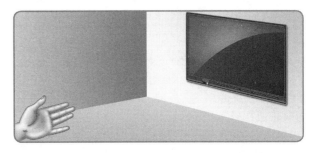

6 .... is an interactive whiteboard.

Vocabulary • Objects

★ **1** Find eight words in the word search. Match the words to the correct pictures (1-8).

1 | 2 | 3 | 4

5 | 6 | 7 | 8

1 *game console*   5 ....
2 ....   6 ....
3 ....   7 ....
4 ....   8 ....

G	A	M	E	C	O	N	S	O	L	E	X
I	F	P	D	J	K	I	L	E	A	Z	M
G	B	3	U	M	B	D	L	Q	Z	W	A
A	M	P	W	T	H	V	V	I	W	A	G
T	P	L	F	P	C	D	W	I	A	T	A
S	K	A	T	E	B	O	A	R	D	C	Z
H	J	Y	C	I	N	A	D	I	S	H	I
I	C	E	S	K	A	T	E	S	T	S	N
Q	K	R	H	P	I	X	Q	G	Y	E	E
S	M	O	C	E	L	L	P	H	O	N	E

★ **2** Put the letters in the correct order.

1 occsmi   *comics*
2 otprse   ....
3 aletwl   ....
4 olptpa   ....
5 aecram   ....
6 igaurt   ....

★ **3** Match the words in Exercise 2 to the pictures.

a 6   b ☐   c ☐

d ☐   e ☐   f ☐

★★ **4** Choose and write the word that doesn't belong.

1 camera   chair   desk   table   *camera*
2 eleven   forty-three   cell phone   twenty-five   ....
3 laptop   ice skates   game console   MP3 player   ....
4 DVD   Spain   Italy   Mexico   ....
5 pen   ruler   skateboard   eraser   ....

★★ **5** Choose a word from box A and a phrase from box B to complete the sentences.

A	comic	~~guitar~~	laptop
	poster	skateboard	watch

B	a big picture	a board with wheels
	a computer	~~a musical instrument~~
	a small clock	a story with superheroes

1 A *guitar is a musical instrument.*
2 A .... is ....
3 A .... is ....
4 A .... is ....
5 A .... is ....
6 A .... is ....

Vocabulary page 104

Reading

★ **1 Read the emails. Write Jon or Megan next to the objects.**

1 *Megan*

2 ....

3 ....

4 ....

5 ....

6 ....

★★ **2 Read the emails again. Match the sentence beginnings (1–5) to the endings (a–e).**

1 *Connect Sports* is *d*
2 Jon is
3 Megan is
4 Miley Cyrus is
5 *Hannah Montana* is

a a fan of Miley Cyrus.
b a TV show about a teenage girl.
c a fan of computer games.
d a game for the computer.
e an actor in *Hannah Montana*.

★★ **3 Read and write true (T), false (F) or don't know (DK).**

1 Jon is a soccer fan. *DK*
2 He's happy because it's his birthday. ....
3 The game is from his brother. ....
4 The Miley Cyrus concert is today. ....
5 Hannah Montana is a pop star at night. ....
6 The photos of Miley are on the table. ....

★★ **4 Answer the questions.**

1 Is the watch from Jon's grandma? *Yes, it is.*
2 Is the book from his friend? ....
3 How many sports are on *Connect Sports*?

   ....
4 Does Megan have a ticket for a Miley Cyrus concert? ....
5 Are the photos of Miley Cyrus from magazines? ....

New Message

Send

Hi Megan,

How are you? I'm really happy because it's my birthday today. I got a watch from my grandma, a book from my brother and a wallet from my friend, Liam. The watch is blue, and the wallet's brown. My favorite present is from my mom and dad. It's a computer game, *Connect Sports*. It's amazing. It has soccer and volleyball, and four other sports. All my family are fans of the game. It's time to go because my friends are here, and my party is about to begin.

Jon

New Message

Send

Hi Jon,

Happy Birthday! Today's a good day for me too because I have a ticket for a Miley Cyrus concert tonight. I'm a Miley Cyrus fan. Miley is the star of *Hannah Montana*, a TV show about a girl who goes to school during the day but is a pop star at night. I have Hannah Montana DVDs and a lot of songs on my MP3 player. On my bedroom walls, I have posters and photos of Miley from magazines. It's five o'clock now and the concert is at seven. Time to get ready!

Megan

Grammar • Have

★ **1 Choose the correct options.**

1 We *have* / *has* our skateboards for the park.
2 He *don't have* / *doesn't have* a poster of the Cowboys football team on the wall.
3 My parents *have* / *has* a big car.
4 She *have* / *has* an autograph book with a lot of famous names in it.
5 I *don't have* / *doesn't have* my cell phone with me.

2 Complete the questions and answers with *do/don't* or *does/doesn't*.

1 Do you have your camera?   Yes, I *do*.
2 .... you and Wendy have your ice skates?   Yes, we do.
3 .... she have her lunch?
No, she doesn't.
4 Do Ed and Paul have a game console?
No, they ....
5 Does your dad have his laptop with him?
Yes, he ....

3 Look at the pictures and complete the sentences. Use the correct form of *have*.

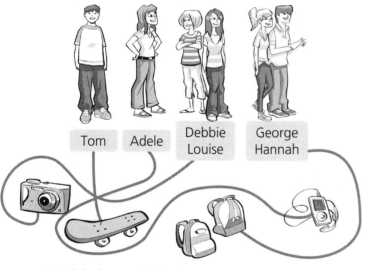

Tom   Adele   Debbie Louise   George Hannah

1 Adele *has* an MP3 player.
2 Debbie and Louise .... a skateboard.
3 Tom .... a camera.
4 George and Hannah .... backpacks.
5 Tom .... a skateboard.
6 Debbie and Louise .... a camera.

4 Look at the list and write Mohammed's sentences.

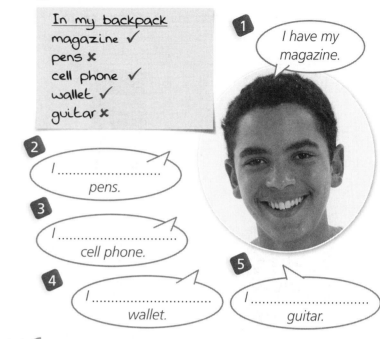

In my backpack
magazine ✓
pens ✗
cell phone ✓
wallet ✓
guitar ✗

1 I have my magazine.

2 I .... pens.

3 I .... cell phone.

4 I .... wallet.

5 I .... guitar.

5 Write questions. Then look at the pictures and answer the questions.

1 he / a guitar
Does he have a guitar?   Yes, he does.
2 they / laptops
....
....
3 she / a watch
....
....
4 it / a ball
....
....
5 he / a cell phone
....
....
6 they / skateboards
....
....

Grammar Reference pages 86–87

Vocabulary • Adjectives

★ **1** Read and choose the correct options.

1 It's my birthday today. I have a new bike.

a ☐   b ☑

2 This show is very interesting.

a ☐   b ☐

3 This puzzle isn't difficult. It's really easy.

a ☐   b ☐

4 **A** I have that cell phone. It's very cheap.
   B Yes, it isn't expensive. It's great.

a ☐   b ☐

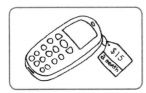 

5 I don't have a big family, so we have a small car.

a ☐   b ☐

Brain Trainer

Learn opposite adjectives in pairs.
Now do Exercise 2.

★ **2** Write the opposite adjectives. Use these words.

bad	boring	cheap
easy	~~old~~	unpopular

1 new   *old*
2 interesting   ....
3 popular   ....
4 difficult   ....
5 good   ....
6 expensive   ....

★★ **3** Complete the sentences with these words.

~~boring~~	difficult	expensive
good	new	popular

1 This book isn't interesting. It's *boring*.
2 That hotel isn't cheap. It's really ....
3 I have a lot of homework today, and it's

....
4 My dad has an old laptop, but mom's laptop is

....
5 Mr. Brown's a very unpopular teacher,
   but Ms. Scarlett is ....
6 It isn't a bad movie. It's ....

★★ **4** Choose the correct options.

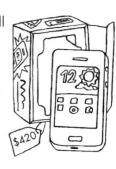

My dad has a ¹(new)/ easy cell
phone. A lot of people have
the same cell. It's ² popular /
old because it's very ³ bad /
good. It's also ⁴ small / boring
and really ⁵ easy / unpopular
to use. He's happy. My mom
isn't happy because it's very
⁶ interesting / expensive.

★★★ **5** Complete the sentences with your own ideas.

1 *Cell phones* are expensive.
2 .... is a good movie.
3 .... is a popular singer.
4 .... is a boring TV show.
5 .... is a big country.
6 .... are old.
7 .... is a difficult subject.
8 .... are small animals.

Vocabulary page 104

Speaking and Listening

★ **1** **Listen and read the conversation.**
3 **Underline** the prepositions of place.

Frank	This is my classroom. We have a new interactive whiteboard.
Beth	Great. Where's your desk?
Frank	It's <u>behind</u> Laura's. Her desk is in front of my desk.
Beth	Is it the desk next to the window?
Frank	Yes, it has a ruler on it, and my backpack is under the chair.
Beth	You have a lot in your backpack. What's in it?
Frank	Pens, pencils, books and my cleats.
Beth	Why do you have cleats in your backpack?
Frank	They're my soccer cleats. I have a soccer game now. Let's go.
Beth	OK.

★ **2** **Read the conversation again. Answer the questions.**

1 Where are Frank and Beth?
They're in the classroom.
2 Where's Frank's desk?
....
3 Where's Laura's desk?
....
4 Where's the ruler?
....
5 Where's Frank's backpack?
....
6 Where are Frank's soccer cleats?
....

★★ **3** **Look at the picture. Complete the sentences with these words.**

~~behind~~	in	in front of	next to	on	under

1 The table is *behind the guitar.*
2 The comics are ....
3 The skateboard is ....
4 The ice skates are ....
5 The backpack is ....
6 The boy is ....

★★ **4** **Listen and choose the correct options.**
4

Frank	Mom, where's my cell phone?
Mom	Is it [1] (*on*) / *under* the table?
Frank	No, it isn't. And it isn't [2] *behind* / *next to* the TV.
Mom	Is it [3] *in* / *under* your bed?
Frank	No, it isn't there.
Mom	Where's your backpack?
Frank	It's [4] *behind* / *on* the door.
Mom	Is it [5] *in* / *next to* your backpack?
Frank	Oh yes. Here it is. Thanks, Mom.

★★ **5** **Read the conversation again. Where's Frank's cell phone?**

★★ **6** **Think of an object in your bedroom. Write a conversation between you and your mom about where it is. Use the model in Exercise 4.**

Speaking and Listening page 113

Grammar • Possessive adjectives and Possessive 's

★ 1 Rewrite the sentences with the apostrophes in the correct place.

1 Here is the cats dinner.
   Here is the cat's dinner.

2 Do you have Johns magazines?

....

3 That is my parents laptop.

....

4 Those are Amandas DVDs.

....

5 When is Bens moms birthday?

....

Brain Trainer

With a new grammar point, memorize the new words or structures as a group.

Write the possessive adjectives for each pronoun.

I	*my*	it	....
you	....	we	....
he	....	they	....
she	....		

Now do Exercise 2.

★ 2 Choose the correct options.

1 It's a friendly dog. (His) / Their name is Sunny.
2 You have an English class now. Do you have *its* / *your* books?
3 My brother and I have basketball posters. *Our* / *Your* favorite team is the Knicks.
4 She doesn't have an expensive cell phone. *Her* / *My* phone is cheap.
5 They're tall children. *Their* / *Your* parents are tall.
6 I have a big bedroom. *His* / *My* bed is next to the window.

★★ 3 Complete the sentences.

1 It's *Ella's* (Ella) bag.
2 They're .... (Charlie) books.
3 This is .... (Jenny and Ed) dog.
4 She has .... (her mom) camera.
5 Is it .... (your parents) car?

★★ 4 Complete the conversation with these words.

| her | his | its | ~~my~~ | our | their | your |

Ed Hello. I'm Ed.
Jo Hi, Ed. [1] *My* name's Jo. Are you here with [2] .... family?
Ed No, I'm not. This is my friend Susie and [3] .... brother. [4] .... name is Adam.
Jo Do they have a dog? Is that [5] .... dog in that bag?
Ed No, it isn't, but we have [6] .... picnic lunch in that bag!
Jo Look! Is that [7] .... ball?
Ed Yes, it is. Let's throw it.
Jo Get the ball! Good dog.
Ed Thanks, Jo.

★★ 5 Look at the pictures and write sentences.

1 autograph book
   It's Jane's autograph book.

2 backpacks

....
....

3 bedroom

....
....

4 notebooks

....
....

Grammar Reference pages 86–87

Reading

1 **Read the text quickly. Match the photos to the descriptions.**

← → C ⌂   ⊗

1 Photo *c*

This awesome red-and-white skateboard is new. It's 75 cm long, and it has black wheels. It's for children over ten years old, and it has a DVD with skateboarding lessons. Now only $35.

2 Photo .....

For all Justin Bieber fans, here are some special items for your collection: a Justin Bieber poster for your wall, his *My World* and *Under the Mistletoe* CDs, and a really cool photo of Justin with his autograph! All for $60.

3 Photo .....

Here is a great collection of 20 comics from 2008 to 2011, including many of the popular *Fantastic Four* and *Commando* comics. They're really good, and they have a lot of exciting stories and pictures. Buy them all for $8.

4 Photo .....

This small blue guitar is in very good condition. It has a black bag, a music book and a DVD. This guitar is expensive when new, but here it's only $37.

2 **Read the descriptions again. Write the correct object below the sentences.**

1 It has his autograph on it.
   Justin Bieber photo
2 It's thirty-seven dollars.
   ....
3 It has a DVD with skateboarding lessons.
   ....
4 It has a music book with it.
   ....
5 They're eight dollars.
   ....

3 **Read the descriptions again. Answer the questions.**

1 Is the skateboard old? *No, it isn't.*
2 Is the poster of Justin Bieber?
   ....
3 Are the DVDs for Justin Bieber fans?
   ....
4 Are the comics new?
   ....
5 Are the *Commando* comics popular?
   ....
6 Is the guitar big?
   ....
7 Does the guitar have a blue bag?
   ....

Listening

1 **Listen and choose the correct option.**
5

Who is Kim's favorite actor?
a Zac Efron
b Leonardo DiCaprio
c Daniel Radcliffe

2 **Listen again. Choose the correct options.**
5

1 Kim has a new (poster) / camera.
2 She has *two / three High School Musical* DVDs.
3 Zac's in *Hairspray / The Karate Kid*.
4 Kim has Zac's songs on her *laptop / MP3 player*.
5 Zac is a *singer and dancer / DJ*.

3 **Listen again. Answer the questions.**
5

1 Is the poster in a bag?
   Yes, it is.
2 Is the poster for Kim's bedroom?
   ....
3 Are the *High School Musical* movies popular?
   ....
4 Does Kim have the *17 Again* DVD?
   ....
5 Do the *High School Musical* movies have a lot of songs in them?
   ....

Writing • A personal profile

1 Rewrite the sentences. Use capital letters, periods and apostrophes.

1 its a nice bedroom
   It's a nice bedroom.

2 helens room has pink walls

....

3 her rooms window is small

....

4 shes a selena gomez fan

....

5 she doesnt have a lot of magazines

....

6 helens family is in the photo

....

2 Read the description of Helen's bedroom and find the false sentence in Exercise 1.

My bedroom

My room is very nice. It has a small window and yellow walls. I have a table next to my bed, a closet with all my clothes, a desk and a chair.

All my favorite things are in my bedroom. I'm a big Selena Gomez fan, and I have a poster of her on my wall. My collection of magazines and my MP3 player are on my desk. I also have a photo of my family on the table next to my bed.

3 Read the description again. Look at the table and write sentences.

The table			the closet.
Her clothes		in	the bed.
The poster	is	on	the wall.
Her MP3 player	are	next to	the desk.
The photo			the table.

1 *The table is next to the bed.*

2 ....

3 ....

4 ....

5 ....

4 Think about your bedroom. Answer the questions.

1 What color is your bedroom?

....

2 Is your room big or small?

....

3 What furniture (bed, table, etc.) is in your room?

....

4 What is on the walls?

....

5 What objects do you have in your room?

....

5 Write two paragraphs about your bedroom. Use the model in Exercise 2 and the information in Exercise 4.

Paragraph 1
Describe your bedroom and the furniture.

Paragraph 2
Write what is in your room.

My room is ....

....

....

....

....

....

....

....

....

....

....

....

Around Town

Vocabulary • Places in a town

★ **1** Complete the puzzle. Find the hidden place.

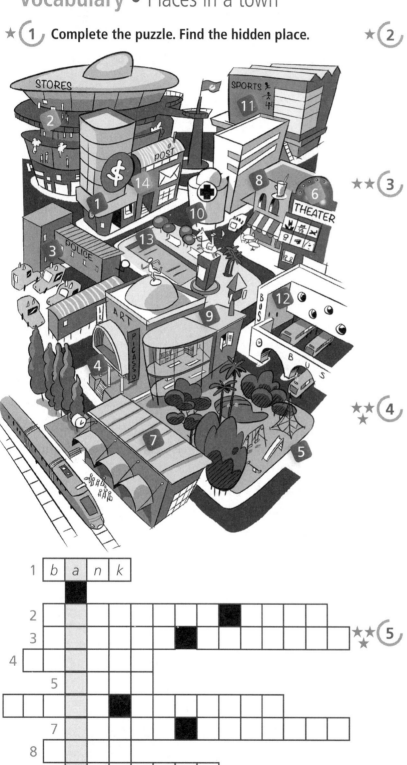

★ **2** Match the words to make four places. Then look at the picture in Exercise 1 and write the correct number.

1 town	a station	☐
2 post	b square	☐
3 bus	c complex	☐
4 sports	d office	☐

★★ **3** Look at the picture in Exercise 1. Complete the sentences with these words.

| bank | ~~police station~~ | movie theater |
| hospital | library | train station |

1 The town square is behind the *police station*.
2 The post office is next to the ....
3 The park is in front of the ....
4 The sports complex is behind the ....
5 The museum is next to the ....
6 The café is next to the ....

★★ **4** Put the words in the correct order.

1 square / in / it's / town / No, / the
   No, it's in the town square.
2 me, / is / bank / here / Excuse / the / near / ?
   ....
3 hospital / it / the / Is / behind / ?
   ....
4 much / you / Thank / very
   ....
5 the / next / it's / office / Yes, / post / to
   ....

★★ **5** Number the sentences from Exercise 4 in the correct order.

Paul 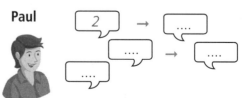 Jen

Vocabulary page 105

Reading

★ 1 **Read the postcard. Mark the places in Hull.**

1 bank	☐	7 museum	☐
2 movie theater	☐	8 restaurant	☐
3 library	☐	9 post office	☐
4 sports complex	☐	10 park	☐
5 town square	☐	11 shopping mall	☐
6 supermarket	☐	12 café	☐

★ 2 **Read the postcard again. Write the correct places.**

> the banks   the café   the hotel
> the park   ~~the supermarket~~

1 It's in the town square.   *the supermarket*
2 It's next to the post office.   ....
3 They are in the town square.   ....
4 It's in front of the hotel.   ....
5 It's behind the hotel.   ....

★★ 3 **Are the statements true (T) or false (F)?**

1 Hull is next to the ocean.   *T*
2 Hull doesn't have a beach.   ....
3 Hull has a shopping mall.   ....
4 The town has an Italian restaurant
   in the town square.   ....
5 There are a lot of seagulls in Hull.   ....
6 The café has delicious pizzas.   ....

★★ 4 **Answer the questions.**

1 Is Josh in Hull with his family?
   Yes, he is.
2 Is it hot and sunny in Hull?
....
3 Is Hull a small town?
....
4 Is the beach behind the hotel?
....
5 Is the hotel next to a bank?
....
6 Is the ice cream good?
....

Hi Chris,
How are you? I'm in Hull with my family. Hull is a seaside town with a great beach.
We're here on vacation, but the weather is terrible. There isn't much to do here when
the weather's bad. It's a small town. There aren't any museums or movie theaters.
There isn't a library, a sports complex or a shopping mall. There are some stores
in the town square. There's also a supermarket, two banks, an Italian restaurant
(they have delicious pizzas) and two post offices. Our hotel is next to a post office.
Behind the hotel, there are a few houses, a park and then the beach. There are a lot
of seagulls in this town!
In front of the hotel, there's a very good café. We have lunch there every day.
The chocolate ice cream is great. How is your vacation?
See you next week.
Love from Josh

Grammar • There is/There are; Some/Any

★ 1 Read the text. Mark the places in the town.

a ☐ b ☐ c ☐ d ☐

e ☐ f ☐ g ☐ h ☐

In my town, there's a bus station, but there isn't a train station. There are two cafés, but there aren't any restaurants. My favorite café is next to the post office. There isn't a supermarket, but there are some small stores. There's a police station. My house is in the center of town. It's next to a beautiful park.

★ 2 Choose the correct options.

1 *There's* / *There are* a bus station in the town.
2 **A** *Is there* / *Are there* a café at the train station?
   B No, *there aren't* / *there isn't.*
3 Are there *any* / *some* old stores in the town square?
4 There are *any* / *some* big trees in the park.

★★ 3 Complete the sentences with *There is*/*There are* (✓) or *There isn't*/*There aren't* (✗).

1 *There is* a new TV show about sports. ✓
2 .... any comics in my backpack. ✗
3 .... a cell phone on the table. ✗
4 .... some magazines under my bed. ✓
5 .... a camera in my backpack. ✓
6 .... any posters on the walls. ✗

★★ 4 Look at the picture. Make sentences with these words.

	some pretty	tree
	a small	flowers
There's	three	dog
There are	a big	bikes
	two	people
	one	guitar

1 *There are some pretty flowers.*
2 ....
3 ....
4 ....
5 ....
6 ....

★★ 5 Write the questions. Then look at the picture in Exercise 4 and answer.

1 any birds?
   Are there any birds?
   Yes, there are.
2 a cat?
   ....
   ....
3 any magazines?
   ....
   ....
4 a swimming pool?
   ....
   ....
5 any lawn chairs?
   ....
   ....
6 a house?
   ....
   ....

Grammar Reference pages 88–89

Vocabulary • Action verbs

★ 1 **Put the letters in the correct order. Then mark the correct pictures.**

1 wsmi   *swim*
2 gjuleg   ....
3 adcne   ....
4 tsaek   ....
5 bcilm   ....
6 eibk   ....

1 **a** ☑   **b** ☐

2 **a** ☐   **b** ☐

3 **a** ☐   **b** ☐

4 **a** ☐   **b** ☐

5 **a** ☐   **b** ☐

6 **a** ☐   **b** ☐

★ 2 **Match the activities to the pictures you didn't mark in Exercise 1.**

| fly | jump | play | ~~run~~ | sing | walk |

1 *run*   4 ....
2 ....   5 ....
3 ....   6 ....

★★ 3 **Find and write the activities.**

lunch (skate) park cat bike
walk fish eraser cheap juggle
camera swim sing comics hospital

1 *skate*   4 ....
2 ....   5 ....
3 ....   6 ....

Brain Trainer

English spelling can be difficult. Learn the pronunciation <u>and</u> the spelling of each new word. Do you say these words as you write them?
walk   talk   climb

Now do Exercise 4.

★★ 4 **Circle the words with a silent letter and write the letter. Then listen and check.**
6

(walk)   *l*   guitar   ....
bike   ....   talk   ....
climb   ....   know   ....
skate   ....   dance   ....

★★ 5 **Complete the phrases with these words. Then add your own ideas.**

| the guitar | a kite | a race |
| six oranges | ~~a song~~ | a tree |

1 sing *a song, the words*
2 fly .... , ...
3 run .... , ...
4 climb .... , ...
5 juggle .... , ...
6 play .... , ...

Vocabulary page 105

Speaking and Listening

★ ① Match the words and phrases.

1 Be   a shout!
2 Please   b me!
3 Don't   c for us!
4 Wait   d in the street.
5 Watch   e careful!
6 Don't play   f don't do that!

★ ② Read and listen to the conversation. <u>Underline</u>
7 and write the orders and warnings.

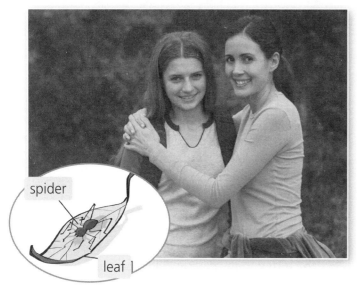

spider

leaf

Mom	It's a beautiful day. We can walk to the lake and have lunch there. There's a café next to the lake.
Beth	Mom, there's a spider on your head!
Mom	Oh no! <u>Help!</u>
Beth	Don't shout! Don't touch it!
Mom	Please help me. I don't like spiders.
Beth	Don't move! Be quiet!
Mom	Come on, Beth. Where is it?
Beth	I don't know. I can't see it now.
Mom	But what's this? This isn't a spider. It's a leaf!
Beth	Sorry, Mom. You're right. It's only a leaf.

1 *Help!*
2 ....
3 ....
4 ....
5 ....

★★ ③ Complete the conversation with these phrases.
8 Then listen and check.

~~Come here, Mom.~~	Don't play with it!
Don't shout!	Don't stand in front of it.
Look!	

Beth	¹ *Come here, Mom.*
Mom	What is it, Beth?
Beth	² .... There's a hedgehog!
Mom	Shh! ³ .... It's asleep!
Beth	It isn't asleep now.
Mom	⁴ .... It isn't a pet.
Beth	It can walk very quickly!
Mom	Yes, it can. ⁵ .... It wants to go that way.
Beth	It's in the tall grass now. That's a really good place for it.
Mom	Yes, it is.

★★★ ④ Look at the picture and write a conversation
between you and a friend. Use the conversation
in Exercise 3 as your model. Use your own ideas,
or the warnings below.

Be quiet!
Be careful!
Don't touch it.
Don't go near it.
Don't move.

....
....
....
....

Speaking and Listening page 114

Grammar • Can/Can't for ability

★ **1** Complete the sentences with *can* or *can't* and one of these verbs.

| climb | fly | ~~jump~~ | skateboard | walk |

1 The dog *can jump* very high.
2 The boy ....
3 The cat .... a tree.
4 The girl .... a kite.
5 The baby ....

★ **2** Complete the answers.

1 **A** Can you skate?
  B No, *I can't.*
2 **A** Can you run a kilometer?
  B Yes, ...
3 **A** Can your dog swim?
  B Yes, ...
4 **A** Can they dance well?
  B No, ...
5 **A** Can your dad juggle?
  B No, ...
6 **A** Can she climb that mountain?
  B Yes, ...

★★ **3** What can Laura do? Complete the sentences.

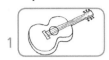 1 ✓
Laura *can* play the guitar.

 2 ✗
She .... sing opera.

 3 ✓
.... ride a bike.

 4 ✗
.... skate.

 5 ✗
.... juggle four balls.

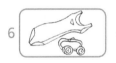 6 ✓
.... swim.

★★★ **4** Put the words in the correct order to make questions. Then answer the questions.

1 you / Can / 100 meters? / run
  Can you run 100 meters?
  Yes, I can. / No, I can't.
2 the / your / play / dad / guitar? / Can
  ....
  ....
3 Can / dance? / your / sing / mom / and
  ....
4 your / skate? / you / and / Can / friends
  ....
  ....
5 mountain? / you / a / a / or / tree / Can / climb
  ....
  ....

Grammar Reference pages 88–89

Reading

1 Read the text quickly. Mark the correct picture.

18

Sasha and Alex are at the train station. It's late, and there are some bad men in the train station, too. They can see the men in front of a café, but the men can't see them.

Sasha and Alex can't go to a hotel because they don't have any money, but Alex has an idea. His aunt has a house in the town. The house is next to a toy museum. There's a map of the town on the wall next to the ticket office. They can find the directions and walk to his aunt's house.

It's a big town. There are a lot of streets and houses. There are also two or three shopping malls and a large park. There's a sports complex in the park. Sasha and Alex can find the police station, the bus station, the town square and some schools on the map, but they can't find the museum. Suddenly, Sasha sees it. At the same moment, they can hear one of the men behind them. They run.

2 Read the text again. Match the sentence beginnings (1–5) to the endings (a–e).

1 Sasha and Alex are at the *d*
2 The men are in front of a
3 The map is next to the
4 Alex's aunt's house is next to the
5 There's a sports complex in the

a museum.
b ticket office.
c park.
d train station.
e café.

3 Answer the questions.

1 Is it early in the morning? *No, it isn't. It's late.*
2 Can Sasha and Alex see the bad men?
....
3 Can they go to Alex's aunt's house?
....
4 Are there any mountains on the map?
....
5 Is there a police station on the map?
....

Listening

> **Brain Trainer**
>
> Don't worry if you don't understand everything you hear. Guess what the person says.
>
> Now do Exercise 1.

1 Listen to Tom and Maddy. Mark the places you hear.

9

1 movie theater ☐   5 bank ☐
2 library ☐   6 park ☐
3 police station ☐   7 train station ☐
4 museum ☐

2 Listen again. Choose the correct options.

9
1 Maddy has the (map) / camera.
2 They're next to a *bus station / police station*.
3 The statue's in front of a *museum / park*.
4 Maddy can see a *library / train station*.
5 The movie theater's *on the next street / in the shopping mall*.

3 Answer the questions.

1 Is Maddy tired? *Yes, she is.*
2 Does Tom have the map?
....
3 Does Maddy have a camera in her backpack?
....
4 Is there a statue of a horse?
....
5 Where are Tom and Maddy?
....
6 Does Tom have the movie tickets?
....

Writing • A description of a town

1 Complete the sentences with *and, or, but*.

1 There's a café *and* two restaurants in the town.
2 There isn't a sports complex .... a swimming pool near my house.
3 She can't sing, ... she can dance really well.
4 There are a lot of small stores, ... there isn't a supermarket.
5 You can swim in a swimming pool .... the ocean.
6 I can juggle, ... I can ride a unicycle.

2 Complete the text with these words.

afternoon	and	~~bike~~	can	interesting
mall	or	station	theater	

A day trip to Stratford

In the morning, we can [1] *bike* to the town square. There's a big shopping [2] .... next to the police [3] .... It has a lot of cool stores.
In the [4] .... , we can visit the museum. It's expensive, but it's very [5] .... There are statues, posters, old books [6] .... some beautiful paintings. There's a wonderful painting of some people in a café. It's my favorite.
In the evening, we [7] .... go to an Italian restaurant, [8] .... we can watch a movie at the movie [9] ....

3 Read the description in Exercise 2 and write the places.

1 *town square*   5 ....
2 ....   6 ....
3 ....   7 ....
4 ....   8 ....

4 Look at the brochure. Mark the things you can do in Charlton.

☐ go shopping
☐ skateboard in the park
☐ visit the museum
☐ watch a movie at the theater
☐ play sports
☐ swim in the pool
☐ have lunch in a Chinese restaurant
☐ have dinner in a French restaurant

5 Now write a description of Charlton. Use the model in Exercise 2 and the ideas in Exercise 4.

A day trip to Charlton

In the morning, we can ....
....
In the afternoon, ...
....
In the evening, ...
....
....

3 School Days

Vocabulary • Daily routines

Brain Trainer

Learn words that go together:
get dressed   have breakfast   watch TV

Now do Exercise 1.

★ **1** Match the words to make daily routines.

1 I meet — a my homework.
2 We start — b my friends.
3 I clean up — c my teeth.
4 We have — d my room.
5 I brush — e lunch.
6 I do — f school.

★ **2** Look at the pictures. Complete the sentences with these phrases.

get dressed   ~~get up~~   go home   go to bed
have breakfast   have dinner   take a shower

Bill

1 I *get up*.
2 I ....
3 I ....
4 I ....

Sam

5 I ....
6 I ....
7 I ....

★★ **3** Look at Exercise 2. Read the sentences and choose the correct name.

1 I get up early.   Sam / (Bill)
2 I have dinner with my family.   Sam / Bill
3 I take a shower in the morning.   Sam / Bill
4 I go to bed at 10 p.m.   Sam / Bill
5 I have breakfast with my sister.   Sam / Bill

★★ **4** Write these words under the correct verb.

dressed   ~~home~~   lunch
to school   breakfast   up

go	have	get
home	....	....
....		

★★ **5** Complete the text with *go, take, have* or *get*.

Every morning, I ¹ *get* up early. I ² ....
a shower, and then I ³ .... dressed.
I ⁴ .... breakfast with my family,
and then I ⁵ .... to school.
We start school at 9 o'clock. At 1 o'clock,
we ⁶ .... lunch. After school,
I ⁷ .... home and do my
homework. I ⁸ .... dinner and
watch TV in the evening. I ⁹ ....
to bed at 10 o'clock.

Vocabulary page 106

Reading

★ **1** Read the magazine article. Mark the activities Antonio does.

1 ☐   4  ☐

2 ☐   5 ☐

3 ☐   6 ☐

★★ **2** Read the article again. Match the sentence beginnings (1–6) to the endings (a–f).

1 Antonio has   a four years old.
2 His sister is   b a tennis coach.
3 Antonio can   c a small family.
4 His mom is   d at the gym.
5 His tennis lessons are   e dinner together.
6 The family has   f play tennis.

★★ **3** Choose the correct options.

1 Antonio *has* / *doesn't have* a big family.
2 His family *likes* / *doesn't like* tennis.
3 He *goes* / *doesn't go* to the gym with his sister.
4 Antonio's stepdad *is* / *isn't* his tennis coach.
5 He *goes* / *doesn't go* home after his tennis lesson.
6 He *goes* / *doesn't go* to bed early.

★★★ **4** Read the article again. Answer the questions.

1 How many people are there in Antonio's family?
There are four people.
2 Can Antonio's sister play tennis?
....
3 Is Antonio's tennis practice before breakfast?
....
4 Is Antonio's tennis lesson after school?
....
5 Does he have a computer in his bedroom?
....
6 Is Antonio tired in the evening?
....

A Day in the Life of
… the Tennis Star, **Antonio Perez!**

I have a small family. There's my mom, my stepdad, my sister and me. We all love tennis—my sister can play tennis, and she's only four years old!

On school days, I get up at 5:30 a.m. and get dressed in my tennis clothes. I have breakfast, and then my mom and I go to the gym together. She works there. I play tennis for an hour before school. After tennis, I take a shower and get dressed in my school uniform. I meet my friends at 8:20 a.m., and we walk to school together. School starts at 9 a.m.

After school, I go to the gym again. I have a tennis lesson at 4:15 p.m. with my mom. She's my tennis coach. Then we go home. My stepdad doesn't get home until 6 p.m. We have dinner together at 6:30 p.m., and then I do my homework. From 7 to 8 p.m., I watch TV or play computer games in my bedroom. I go to bed early because I'm tired—I get up very early in the morning.

Grammar • Present simple: affirmative and negative

★ **1** Complete the sentences with these verbs. Use each verb twice.

do ~~go~~ go have play watch

1 I *go* home after school, but my brother *goes* to the park.
2 I .... on the computer, but my brother .... soccer.
3 I .... eggs for dinner, but my brother .... pizza.
4 I .... my homework in my bedroom, but my brother .... his homework in the living room.
5 I .... old movies on TV, but my brother .... sports.
6 I .... to bed at 9 p.m., but my brother .... to bed at 9:30 p.m.

★ **2** Complete the sentences with *don't/doesn't* and the correct form of the verbs.

1 My friends and I go to the town square on the weekend. We *don't go* to the park.
2 I get up early on school days.
   I .... early on the weekend.
3 My dad takes a shower in the morning.
   He .... a shower in the evening.
4 My sister reads magazines.
   She .... books.
5 Sunita and Raoul play soccer.
   They .... basketball.
6 Our dog likes my friends.
   He .... the mail carrier.

★★ **3** Choose the correct *-s* ending for these verbs. Then listen and check.

10

1 looks	/s/	/z/	/ɪz/
2 goes	/s/	/z/	/ɪz/
3 dances	/s/	/z/	/ɪz/
4 swims	/s/	/z/	/ɪz/
5 meets	/s/	/z/	/ɪz/
6 watches	/s/	/z/	/ɪz/

★★ **4** Complete the description with the Present simple form of the verbs.

Every Saturday morning, I [1] *clean up* (clean up) my room. Lydia, my sister, [2] .... (clean up) her room too, but my room is more messy! Then I [3] .... (clean) out the rabbits' hutches, and Lydia [4] .... (give) the fish some food. After lunch, we [5] .... (go) to the park together. My sister [6] .... (bike), but I [7] .... (walk) because I don't have a bike. We sometimes [8] .... (meet) our friends and [9] .... (play) soccer. In the evening, we [10] .... (not go) out. We [11] .... (watch) TV. I [12] .... (like) game shows, but Lydia [13] .... (not like) them. She [14] .... (like) *The X Factor* and *The Voice*.

★★ **5** Write sentences about the pictures. Use the Present simple affirmative and negative.

1 bike to school / walk
   The students *don't bike to school. They walk.*
2 watch TV / read books
   The girl ....
3 go to the park / play computer games at home
   The boy ....
4 go to the movies / have a picnic
   The friends ....
5 study French / study English
   He ....
6 play soccer / do a puzzle
   I ....

Grammar Reference pages 90–91

Vocabulary • School subjects

★ 1 Read the texts and number the subjects.

a music ☐   d computer science ☐
b math ☐   e French ☐
c PE ☐   f English ☑ 1

1 **Teacher** Good morning, everyone. Open your books to page 27. Today, we are learning the words for school subjects.
2 **Teacher** Simon, what is 128 plus 6 plus 25?
  Boy 159.
  Teacher That's right.
3 **Teacher** Today, we are listening to Beethoven.
4 **Teacher** Today, we are looking at different computer programs.
5 **Teacher** Get ready. Go!
6 **Girl** Bonjour, Madame. Comment allez-vous?
  Teacher Très bien, merci.

★ 2 Complete the crossword with these words.

art   English   geography   history
computer science   literature   math   science

Across

Down

★★ 3 Match the sentence beginnings (1–6) to the subjects (a–f).

1 We write essays about society in e
2 We run and play games in
3 We learn grammar, listen to CDs and talk in pairs in
4 We read about different countries in
5 We learn about computers and how to use them in
6 We work with numbers in

a English.
b math.
c PE.
d computer science.
e social studies.
f geography.

★★ 4 Write the classes.

art   French   literature   music   PE   science

1 We play soccer in the winter and tennis in the summer.   *PE*
2 Our teacher plays the piano and we sing.
....
3 We read a lot of books. My favorite book is *To Kill a Mockingbird*.   ....
4 Our teacher explains the grammar, and we speak in pairs.   ....
5 We look at famous paintings, and then we draw or paint pictures.   ....
6 We learn about the body and plants.
....

★★ 5 Complete the sentences to make them true.

1 I have .... and .... on Wednesday.
2 .... is my geography teacher.
3 I play .... in PE.
4 My science classes are on .... and ....
5 I write essays in ....
6 My favorite subject is ....

Vocabulary page 106

Chatroom Time

Speaking and Listening

★ **(1)** **Listen and read the conversation. <u>Underline</u>**
11 **phrases for asking and answering about time.**

Frank	Let's do our English homework together.
Beth	OK.
Frank	<u>What time is it?</u>
Beth	It's one thirty.
Frank	School gets out at three ten. Can you come to my house at three thirty?
Beth	I can't today because I have a piano lesson.
Frank	What time does your lesson start?
Beth	It's at a quarter to four.
Frank	And what time does it end?
Beth	It's half an hour. It ends at four fifteen.
Frank	Can you come to my house after that?
Beth	Yes, that's fine. I can be there at four forty.
Frank	Good. You can have dinner at my house, and my mom can drive you home at eight o'clock.
Beth	OK. Thanks. See you later.

★ **(2)** **Read the conversation again. Match the times to the activities.**

1 a go home

2 b piano lesson ends

3 c school gets out

4 d piano lesson starts

5 e go to Frank's house

★★ **(3)** **Look at the clocks. Write the times.**

1   2   3   4   5

1 *It's twenty past two.   It's two twenty.*
2 ....
3 ....
4 ....
5 ....

★★ **(4)** **Put the conversation in order.**

a ☐ When does it end?
b ☑ What time is it?
c ☐ What time does it start?
d ☐ OK. Let's watch that.
e ☐ It's twenty past six. What's on TV tonight?
f ☐ It starts at seven o'clock.
g ☐ There's a great monster movie.
h ☐ At eight forty.

★★ **(5)** **Write the conversation from Exercise 4 in order.**
12 **Then listen and check.**

1 *What time is it?*
2 ....
3 ....
4 ....
5 ....
6 ....
7 ....
8 ....

★★ **(6)** **You want to watch TV today. Choose a show from the TV schedule below and write a conversation between you and a friend. Use the model in Exercise 5.**

7:30	**The Simpsons**
7:45	**Movie: The Great Chicken Race**
9:15	**A History of Clocks**
9:45	**The Funny Ha Ha Show**
10:10	**The Sports Quiz**

Speaking and Listening page 115

Grammar • Present simple: questions and short answers

★ (1) **Complete the questions with *Do* or *Does*.**

1 *Do* you know any movie stars?
2 .... she like ice cream?
3 .... they go to the movies every week?
4 .... the movie start at 7:30?
5 .... you and your family play a lot of sports?
6 .... your dad watch TV in the evening?

★ (2) **Match the questions to the answers. Then choose the correct verb.**

1 Do you and your family get up early?   d
2 Do you brush your teeth after breakfast?
3 Does your dad take a shower in the morning?
4 Does your room usually look neat?
5 Does your sister walk to school?
6 Do your mom and dad work together?

a No, they *don't / doesn't*.
b Yes, it *do / does*.
c Yes, she *do / does*.
d No, we *don't* / *doesn't*.
e Yes, I *do / does*.
f No, he *don't / doesn't*.

★★ (3) **Complete the questions with *Do* or *Does*. Then answer the questions.**

1 *Do* you go to school by bus?
   Yes, I do. / No, I don't.
2 .... you and your friends study French at school?   ....
3 .... your English teacher use an interactive whiteboard?   ....
4 .... your friends have lunch at school?
   ....
5 .... your best friend like art?
   ....

★★ (4) **Look at the chart and answer the questions.**

1 Does Jenny have art at nine o'clock?
   Yes, she does.
2 Does Noah have geography at eleven thirty?
   ....
3 Do they have science at a quarter to ten?
   ....
4 Does Noah have music at ten thirty?
   ....
5 Does Jenny have history at eleven thirty?
   ....
6 Does Jenny have English at one fifteen?
   ....

Monday	Noah	Jenny
🕘	math	art
🕤	science	science
🕥	music	math
🕚	history	geography
🕐	computer science	English

★★★ (5) **Write questions with the Present simple of these verbs. Then answer the questions.**

| clean up   get up   go   like   ~~live~~ |

1 you and your family / in a small town?
   Do you and your family live in a small town?
   Yes, we do. / No, we don't.
2 your mom / at 7 a.m.?
   ....
   ....
3 you / your room every day?
   ....
   ....
4 your best friend / animals?
   ....
   ....
5 your parents / to the movies on the weekend?
   ....
   ....

Grammar Reference pages 90–91

Reading

1 Read the text. Choose the correct description.

1 Lance goes to school every day. He has classes with the other students in the classroom.

2 Lance doesn't go to school every day. He has classes with the other students on his computer.

The School of the Air

This is Lance. He's Australian. He doesn't go to school because there isn't a school where he lives. Australia is a very big country, and he lives on a sheep farm hundreds of kilometers from a town.

Lance studies at home. He has books, pens and pencils, but his classes are on the computer. Every morning, Lance sits in front of his laptop for an hour, and watches and listens to his classes. His teachers use cameras and interactive whiteboards. He can talk to his teacher and the other students in his "class." In the afternoon, Lance does his homework. He emails his homework to his teachers.

A lot of children live on farms and study at home in Australia. Once a year, the students in each "class" meet. Lance flies to a school in Port Macquarie and stays there for a week. He and the other students go on trips, and there's also a Sports Day. It's a great week, and it's the only time he sees the other students.

2 Read the text again. Are the statements true (T) or false (F)?

1 Lance lives on a sheep farm in Australia.   *T*

2 He walks to school every day.   ....

3 The teachers use cameras and interactive whiteboards.   ....

4 He doesn't have any homework.   ....

5 Lance stays at a school in Port Macquarie for two weeks.   ....

6 There's a Sports Day for the class once a year.   ....

3 Answer the questions.

1 Why does Lance study at home?
There isn't a school where he lives.

2 Are Lance's classes in the morning?
....

3 Does Lance talk to the other students?
....

4 Does Lance mail his homework to his teachers?
....

5 Do many children study at home in Australia?
....

6 Does Lance fly to Port Macquarie?
....

Listening

1 Listen to a radio interview. Mark the correct picture.

13   Where does Darren study?

1 ☐   2 ☐   3 ☐

2 Listen again. Choose the correct options.

13

1 Darren *goes / doesn't go* to school.

2 He *has / doesn't have* classes with his parents.

3 He *studies / doesn't study* history.

4 Darren's sisters *play / don't play* the guitar.

5 They *meet / don't meet* other children every week.

3 Listen again. Complete the sentences.

13

1 Darren is *13 years old*.

2 Darren studies with his ....

3 Darren studies the same subjects as ....
....

4 His sisters have ....

5 Darren's guitar lesson is on ....

6 Every week, the home-schooled children go to the swimming pool, a museum or ....
....

Writing • An email

Brain Trainer

When there are simple rules, learn them.

Write *in, on* and *at* in these rules for time phrases:

_____ + day

_____ + the morning / the evening

_____ + time

Now do Exercise 1.

1 Complete the emails with *in*, *on* or *at*.

New Message   ✕

                                              Send

Hi Chris,

Harry Potter is playing at the movie
theater next week. It starts [1] *at* seven
o'clock [2] .... the evening. Are you
free any day? Let me know, and I can get
the tickets.

Fraser

New Message   ✕

                                              Send

Hi Fraser,

Great idea! I can't go [3] ....
Monday because I go swimming
[4] .... six thirty. [5] .... Tuesday,
it's my mom's birthday party [6] ....
the evening. I'm free [7] ....
Wednesday. I can also go [8] ....
Thursday, but I have a guitar lesson
[9] .... 5:20 [10] .... Friday.
Is Wednesday or Thursday good for you
and the others?

Chris

---

2 Read the emails in Exercise 1. Complete Chris's
planner for next week. Then complete it for you.

Monday	*swimming / 6:30*
Tuesday	....
Wednesday	....
Thursday	....
Friday	....

Monday	....
Tuesday	....
Wednesday	....
Thursday	....
Friday	....

3 Write sentences about your week. Use your
planner from Exercise 2.

1 On Monday, I have a ....
2 On Tuesday, ...
3 ....
4 ....
5 ....

4 Write a short email to Fraser. Use the model in
Exercise 1 and your information from Exercises
2 and 3.

Hi Fraser,

Good idea! ....

....

....

....

....

....

....

....

....

....

....

....

....

Check 1

Grammar

1 **Choose the correct options.**

0 He *has* / *have* a party for *our* / *his* birthday.
1 I *has* / *have* a new shirt. I love *its* / *her* color.
2 Tania *has* / *have* a car. *His* / *Her* car is red.
3 We *has* / *have* two laptops at home. They are my *parent's* / *parents'* laptops.
4 This is *John's* / *Johns'* wallet. It *doesn't have* / *don't have* any money in it.
5 My friends *doesn't have* / *don't have* a big yard. *His* / *Their* yard is small.

/ 5 points

2 **What's on the table? Write *There's*/*There isn't*, *There are*/*There aren't* and *a/an*, *some* or *any*.**

0 *There are some* comics.
1 .... camera.
2 .... MP3 player.
3 .... books.
4 .... pens.
5 .... watch.

/ 5 points

3 **Look at the information. Answer the questions.**

	Lizzy	Noah
🥎	✓	✗
🩳 🛼	✗	✓
⛸	✗	✗
🚲	✓	✓
🎹 🎸	✗	✓

0 Can Lizzy juggle?   *Yes, she can.*
1 Can Noah play the piano?
....
2 Can Noah swim?
....
3 Can Noah and Lizzy skate?
....
4 Can Noah and Lizzy bike?
....
5 Can Lizzy play the guitar?
....

/ 5 points

4 **Complete the sentences with the Present simple of the verbs.**

0 We *like* (like) art, and we love (*love*) music.
1 My sisters .... (not play) tennis in PE. They .... (do) gymnastics.
2 I .... (not wear) a green uniform. I .... (wear) a black uniform.
3 My best friend .... (not bike) to school. She .... (walk).
4 .... Mrs. Bagshaw .... (teach) social studies? No, she ....
5 .... classes .... (end) at ten? Yes, they ....

/ 5 points

Vocabulary

5 **Complete the names of the school subjects (1–5). Then match them to the pictures (a–e).**

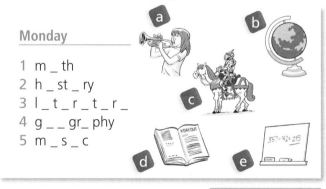

Monday

1 m _ th
2 h _ st _ ry
3 l _ t _ r _ t _ r _
4 g _ _ gr _ phy
5 m _ s _ c

/ 5 points

6 Complete the sentences with places.

0 There are trees in the p*ark*.
1 Let's get a cup of coffee at the c ....
2 There are a lot of old statues in the m ....
3 Doctors work at the h ....
4 People go to the l ....
to borrow books.
5 There's a swimming pool in the
s .... c ....

/ 5 points

Speaking

7 Match the orders (a–f) to the pictures (1–6).
Then complete the orders with these words.

| behin | in | in front of | ~~next to~~ | on | under |

a ☑ Don't play soccer *next to* the street.
b ☐ Don't talk .... the library.
c ☐ Put the bag .... the table.
d ☐ Wait for me .... the movie theater.
e ☐ Don't stand .... the TV.
f ☐ Walk with me .... the umbrella.

/ 5 points

8 Rewrite the text. Write the times in a different way.

Good morning and welcome to the start of the new school year.

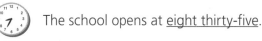 The school opens at <u>eight thirty-five</u>.

The first class starts at <u>nine fifteen</u>.

The morning break is at <u>ten forty-five</u>.

Lunch is at <u>twelve thirty</u>.

The afternoon classes start at <u>two p.m.</u>

School gets out at <u>three ten</u>.

Good morning and welcome to the start of the new school year.
0 The school opens *at twenty-five to nine.*
1 The first class starts ....
2 The morning break is ....
3 Lunch is ....
4 The afternoon classes start ....
5 School gets out ....

/ 5 points

Translation

9 Translate the sentences.

1 He doesn't have his dad's laptop.
....
2 There's a big shopping mall in our town.
....
3 I get up at seven thirty, and then I get dressed.
....
4 Do we have a science class on Thursday?
....
5 She can juggle six balls.
....

/ 5 points

Dictation

10 Listen and write.
14

/ 5 points

Animal Magic

Vocabulary • Unusual animals

★ **1** Label these animals.

> frog giant rabbit hissing cockroach
> ~~piranha~~ pygmy goat

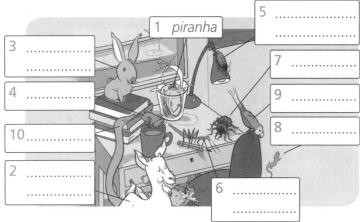

1 *piranha*

3 ....
....

4 ....

5 ....
....

7 ....

9 ....

8 ....

10 ....

2 ....
....

6 ....
....

★ **2** Put the letters in the correct order. Then label the animals in the picture in Exercise 1.

6 tsikc secnti *stick insect*
7 urtaatlan ....
8 iazrdl ....
9 aroprt ....
10 yptohn ....

★★ **3** Read the sentences and choose the correct animal.

1 It's black, and it eats insects.
  (tarantula) / giant rabbit / piranha
2 It's very long, but it can't walk.
  lizard / python / stick insect
3 It's colorful, and it can fly.
  giant rabbit / parrot / lizard
4 It's a farm animal and a popular pet.
  pygmy goat / hissing cockroach / lizard

> **Brain Trainer**
>
> **Learn the common and useful words first. Choose the common word in each pair:**
>
> mammal / dog tarantula / spider
> frog / amphibian fish / piranha
>
> **Now do Exercise 4.**

★★ **4** Complete the table.

	Category	Animal
1	*amphibian*	frog toad
2	....	parrot
3	mammal	....
4	....	lizard ....
5	insect	....
6	fish	....
7	....	tarantula

★★ **5** Complete the sentences with these words.

> frogs insects mammals
> parrots ~~reptiles~~ tarantulas

1 Snakes and lizards are *reptiles*.
2 .... are birds.
3 .... and toads
  are amphibians.
4 Cockroaches are ....,
  and they have six legs.
5 .... are spiders,
  not insects, because they have eight legs.
6 Goats, dogs and cats are all ....

★★★ **6** Complete the dialogue with these words.

> amphibian ~~animals~~ do do lizard reptile

Paul Do you like [1] *animals*?
Jen Yes, I [2] ....
Paul Do you have a pet?
Jen Yes, I [3] .... I like reptiles.
  I have a snake and a [4] ....
  I have a frog, too.
Paul Is that a [5] ....?
Jen No, it's an [6] ....

Vocabulary page 107

Reading

★ **1** Read the blog. One animal is in the photos but not in the blog. Put an ✗ next to the photo.

★★ **2** Read the text again. Are the statements true (T) or false (F)?

1 The school is in a big city.   *F*
2 There are cows on the farm.   ....
3 Susie is eleven years old.   ....
4 Susie usually helps with the goats.   ....
5 The farm sells the eggs and meat.   ....
6 Her favorite animals are the pigs.   ....

★★ **3** Choose the correct options.

1 There are eighty (sheep) / *pigs* on the farm.
2 The farm has two *dogs* / *donkeys*.
3 Susie is in *sixth grade* / *seventh grade*.
4 She *likes* / *doesn't like* the classes on the farm.
5 She likes the *eggs* / *chickens*.
6 The horses are *old* / *big*.

★★★ **4** Answer the questions.

1 Where is the school?
   It's in the country.
2 How many goats are there?
   ....
3 When are Susie's classes on the farm?
   ....
4 What does Susie learn about on the farm?
   ....
5 Why does Susie go to school early?
   ....
6 How does Susie help with the chickens?
   ....

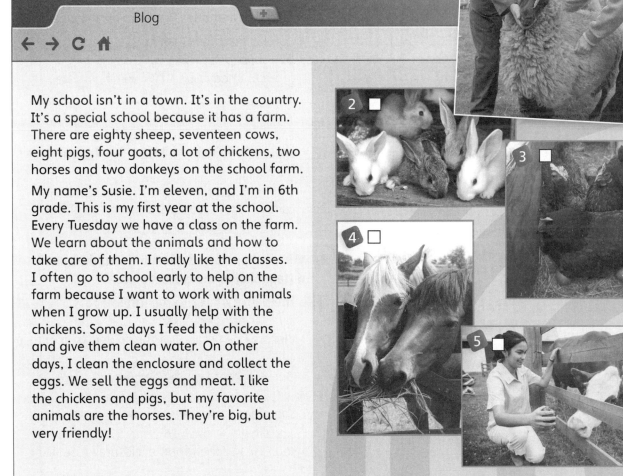

My school isn't in a town. It's in the country. It's a special school because it has a farm. There are eighty sheep, seventeen cows, eight pigs, four goats, a lot of chickens, two horses and two donkeys on the school farm.

My name's Susie. I'm eleven, and I'm in 6th grade. This is my first year at the school. Every Tuesday we have a class on the farm. We learn about the animals and how to take care of them. I really like the classes. I often go to school early to help on the farm because I want to work with animals when I grow up. I usually help with the chickens. Some days I feed the chickens and give them clean water. On other days, I clean the enclosure and collect the eggs. We sell the eggs and meat. I like the chickens and pigs, but my favorite animals are the horses. They're big, but very friendly!

Grammar • Adverbs of frequency

Grammar Reference pages 92–93

★ **1** **Write the words in the correct place.**

always	hardly ever	~~never~~
often	sometimes	usually

0% 25% 50% 60% 80% 100%

1 0%   *never*
2 25%   ....
3 50%   ....
4 60%   ....
5 80%   ....
6 100%   ....

★ **2** **Read the text. Write *Bob* or *Will* next to each picture.**

Bob   ....

....

....

Bob and Will are friends, but they are very different. Bob always gets up early and takes a shower. He sometimes eats cereal for breakfast, and sometimes toast and honey. After breakfast, Bob feeds the cat. He always leaves the house at eight thirty and takes the bus to school. He's never late.

Will hardly ever gets up early, and he never takes a shower in the morning. He always eats cereal for breakfast. He never eats toast and honey. After breakfast, Will sometimes feeds the fish. He usually leaves the house at eight forty and often misses the bus to school. He's often late.

Grammar Reference pages 92–93

Brain Trainer

Always check the word order in your sentences. Remember:

Subject + adverb of frequency + verb
We   never   go to the theater.

but

Subject + verb *to be* + adverb of frequency
He   's   hardly ever late.

Now do Exercise 3.

★★ **3** **Rewrite the sentences with an adverb of frequency. Make the sentences true for you.**

1 I eat breakfast in the morning.
....
2 I'm late for school.
....
3 I help at home.
....
4 I go to the park after school.
....

★★ **4** **Put the words in the correct order to make sentences. What does Penny do on the weekend?**

1 never / She / volleyball / plays
She never plays volleyball.
2 often / Sunday / on / TV / watches / She
....
3 sometimes / the / She / movies / goes / to
....
4 always / on / talks / phone / She / to / friends / her / the
....
5 usually / homework / she / her / do / Does ?
....

★★★ **5** **Write sentences and questions. Put the adverb of frequency in the correct place.**

1 The parrot / talk / to me (often)
The parrot often talks to me.
2 Visitors / be / scared of the spiders (sometimes)
....
3 Our dog / get / on my bed (never)
....
4 She / feed / the cat (always)
....
5 you / clean / the rabbit enclosure? (usually)
....

Grammar • Present simple with *Wh* questions

★① **Read the answers. Choose the correct question words.**

1 *Who /(Where)*is your teacher?
  She's in the library.
2 *Why / How often* do you have English classes?
  We have three classes a week.
3 *Who / What* do you sit next to in class?
  I sit next to Amelia.
4 *How often / Why* are you late?
  Because I missed the bus.
5 *What / When* does the zookeeper feed the rabbits?   He gives them carrots.

★② **Complete the questions with these words.**

| How often | What | When | Where | ~~Who~~ |

1 *Who* is your science teacher?
2 .... homework do you have today?
3 .... do penguins live?
4 .... does the movie start?
5 .... do you play sports?

★★③ **Write the questions.**

1 What animals / you / like?
  What animals do you like?
2 Who / scared of spiders?
  ....
3 How often / you / take your dog for a walk?
  ....
4 Where / pythons / come from?
  ....
5 When / the zookeeper / feed the rabbits?
  ....

★★④ **Write the questions for these answers.**

1 *What is your favorite football team?*
  My favorite football team is the Cowboys.
2 ....
  My English teacher is Ms. Barber.
3 ....
  My school is next to the park.
4 ....
  My birthday is June 26.
5 ....
  My teacher is hardly ever out of town.

Grammar Reference pages 92–93

Vocabulary • Parts of the body

★① **Match the pictures to the descriptions.**

1 It has a small head. It has three black paws and one white paw. It has a long tail.   *d*
2 It has a long white neck, white wings, an orange beak and black feet.
3 It has a small head, six thin legs and a long, thin tail, but it doesn't have wings.
4 It has two arms and legs. It has two hands and feet. It has ten fingers and toes.

★② **Match the sentence halves 1–5 to a–e.**

1 A lizard has   a four paws.
2 A tarantula has   b two wings and a beak.
3 A rabbit has   c fins.
4 A parrot has   d a long tail.
5 A fish has   e eight legs and feet.

★★③ **Put the letters in the correct order.**

1 A python has a long body and a small *head* (deha), but it doesn't have a *neck* (knce).
2 We have ten .... (nifgsre) and ten .... (oste).
3 Fish have a body, ... (nifs) and a .... (lait).
4 Parrots have a .... (akbe) and colorful .... (sigwn).
5 Dogs have four .... (gels) and .... (waps).

★★④ **Write about yourself using these words.**

| arms | feet | fingers | hands | head |
| legs | neck | toes | wings | |

I have ....
....
....
....
....
....
....

Vocabulary page 107

Chatroom Likes and dislikes

Speaking and Listening

★ **1** Mark the sentences about likes.

1 That dog's very dirty. ☐
2 Rex hates taking a shower. ☐
3 He loves running around the yard. ☐
4 He doesn't like swimming. ☐
5 He likes hiding things. ☐
6 He's a very friendly dog. ☐

★ **2** Read and listen to the conversation.
15 Mark the things Rex likes.

Beth	Hi, Mom. I'm back. Frank's here, too.
Mom	Hello, Frank. The dog's very dirty, Beth. Can you clean him, please?
Beth	But Mom, Rex hates getting a bath.
Mom	I know, but he can go outside after his bath. He loves running around the yard.
Beth	Rex hates water. He doesn't like swimming, and he never goes in the river.
Frank	Does he like playing with a ball?
Beth	No, not really. He likes hiding things. He often hides our stuff in the yard.
Frank	He's a very friendly dog.
Beth	Yes. He likes sitting next to me in the evening.

1 ☐   2 ☐   3 ☐

4 ☐   5 ☐   6 ☐

★★ **3** Complete the conversation with these words.
16 Then listen and check.

cook	eat	play sports
~~play tennis~~	run	watch TV

Ali	What do you like doing in your free time?
Liz	I love ¹ 🎾 *playing tennis.*
Ali	So do I. I like ² 🏃 .... , too.
Mia	I don't like ³ ⚽ .... I like ⁴ 📺 ....
Ali	You like ⁵ 🍳 .... , too. I love ⁶ 🍽 .... your food.
Mia	That's true. Thank you, Ali.

★★ **4** Write true sentences about yourself. Use *love, like, don't like* and *hate*.

1 bike

....

2 eat eggs

....

3 watch sports on TV

....

4 listen to music

....

5 clean up my room

....

★★ **5** Look at the table. Write a conversation between Jo and Simon. Use the model in Exercise 3.

	Likes	Doesn't like
Jo	biking	reading
	going to the movies	
	listening to music	
Simon	biking	listening to music
	reading	singing
	running	

Speaking and Listening page 116

Grammar • Must/Mustn't

1 c ☐

2 ☐ ☐

3 ☐ ☐

a You mustn't run across the street.
b You mustn't go to school.
c You must stay in bed.
d You must be quiet.
e You must look left and right.
f You mustn't write in the books.

★ **2** Complete the sentences with *must* or *mustn't*.

1 We *mustn't* arrive late for school.
2 They .... be good to animals.
3 He .... hurt other people.
4 You .... shout at the children.

★★ **3** Put the words in the correct order. Then answer the question below.

1 late / You / be / mustn't
You mustn't be late.
2 the / mustn't / classroom / eat / in / He
....
3 a / They / wear / uniform / must
....
4 phones / use / mustn't / cell / our / We
....
5 She / listen / teacher / to / must / the
....
Where are they? ....
....

★★ **4** Complete the sentences with these phrases and *must* or *mustn't*.

| buy a ticket | clean up my room | close the gates |
| ~~litter~~ | stand on her desk | talk |

1 You *mustn't litter* in the park. ✗
2 They ....
on the farm. ✓
3 We ....
in the library. ✗
4 She ....
at school. ✗
5 I ....
at home. ✓
6 You ....
on the bus. ✓

★★ **5** Write sentences about the park rules. Use a word or phrase from each box.

| You | must mustn't | ~~pick~~ write climb keep put | the trees. on the statues. ~~the flowers.~~ your dog on a leash. litter in a trash can. |

1 *You mustn't pick the flowers.*
2 ....
3 ....
4 ....
5 ....

Grammar Reference pages 92–93

Reading

1 Read the article quickly. Choose the correct answer.

What does Jack Stone do? He's a …
a zookeeper.   b photographer.
c teacher.   d farmer.

Jack Stone doesn't have a pet, but he has a lot of pictures of animals because he's a photographer. He takes photos of pets. He is very good, and his photos are often in the newspapers. He also has photos on his website. There are a lot of cats and dogs, but there are other pets too—horses, rabbits, guinea pigs, parrots and fish.

Jack explains, "People usually bring their pet to my studio, but sometimes I go to the pet's home to take the photos. I like the pets to be happy, or the photos aren't good. I often take the photos outside because animals like being outside. I like finding the right place to photograph the animal. People want photos because they love their pets. Every pet is special. I show their character. My photos show how each animal is different. I like animals, and I like taking photos. I'm lucky because I love my work."

2 Read the article again. Are the statements true (T) or false (F)?

1 Jack has a lot of cats.   F
2 Jack's photos are never in the newspapers.   ....
3 Jack only takes photos of cats and dogs.   ....
4 Jack doesn't always take the photos
   in his studio.   ....
5 Jack wants the pets to be happy.   ....
6 Jack hates taking photos.   ....

3 Answer the questions.

1 What does Jack take photos of?
   He takes photos of pets.
2 Where can you see Jack's photos?
   ....
3 Which animals can you see on his website?
   ....
4 Where does Jack take the photos?
   ....

Listening

1 Listen and mark the correct picture.

17   1 ☐   2 ☐   3 ☐

2 Listen again. Choose the correct answers.

17   1 Every day, Ben takes a photo of a different
         child / child /(animal.)
      2 The unusual pet on his website is a
         stick insect / frog.
      3 There's a funny photo of a *tarantula / parrot.*
      4 The animals hardly ever *run away / bite.*
      5 Ben's favorite photo is of a *goat / python.*

3 Read the answers and write the questions. Then listen again and check.

17

> Are there any funny photos?
> Are there any unusual pets on your website?
> Do the animals bite you?
> What's your favorite photo?
> ~~Are there people in the photos?~~

1 *Are there people in the photos?*
   Not usually.
2 ....
   Yes. There's a photo of a red frog on a twig.
3 ....
   Yes, there are. The photo of a tarantula on
   a man's head is funny.
4 ....
   Hardly ever.
5 ....
   It's a photo of a goat.

Writing • An animal fact sheet

1 Look at the fact sheet and complete the sentences.

Pet Fact Sheet **Stick Insects**

Continent: South America, Asia, Australia
Weight: 65 g
Length: 17 cm
Habitat: trees
Diet: plants, leaves
Abilities: can hide very well

1 Stick insects come from *South America, Asia and Australia.*
2 They grow to .... long, and they weigh ....
3 They live in ....
4 They eat ....
5 They can ....

2 Complete the description with these words.

| apples | backyard | cats | eats | eyes |
| lives | ~~pet~~ | sunny | white | |

3 Complete the table for Emma. Use the information in Exercise 2.

Name	Emma	Polly
Type of animal	[1] *guinea pig*	parrot
Home	[2]	cage
Diet	[3]	bird seed, nuts, fruit
Color	[4]	gray beak, red head and body, blue and yellow wings
Likes & dislikes	[5]	• likes talking and listening to people • doesn't like going to bed late

4 Write a short article about Polly. Use the model from Exercise 2 and the notes in Exercise 3.

....
....
....
....
....
....

My pet's home _____

My [1] *pet* is a guinea pig. Her name is Emma, and she [2] .... in a hutch in the [3] ....

Diet _____

She usually [4] .... special guinea pig food. I sometimes give her [5] .... , too.

Appearance _____

She's brown and [6] .... She has small [7] .... and ears, and a pink nose.

Likes and dislikes _____

She likes [8] .... days because she can run around outside. She doesn't like [9] .... because they want to eat her!

5 Out and About!

Vocabulary • Activities

★ **1** Circle the complete names of the activities.

bowling	climbing	dancing
the flute	gymnastics	hiking
horseback	ice	kayaking
mountain	(painting)	rollerblading
singing	surfing	

★ **2** Write the activities from Exercise 1 under the correct pictures.

1 *painting* 2 .... 3 ....

4 .... 5 .... 6 ....

7 .... 8 .... 9 ....

★ **3** Complete the phrases with the rest of the words in Exercise 1. Then number the pictures.

1 *ice* skating
2 .... riding
3 playing ....
4 .... biking

a ☐ b ☐

c ☐ d ☐

★★ **4** Complete the sentences.

1 I hate [+ *an activity you do outside*]

....

2 I don't like [+ *an activity you do at home*]

....

3 I like [+ *an activity you do on the weekend*]

....

4 I love [+ *a sport*] ....

★ **5** Complete the sentences with these activities.

bowling	dancing
horseback riding	ice skating
kayaking	~~mountain biking~~
painting	play an instrument

1 She has a bike, and she goes *mountain biking* every week.
2 He goes .... with his horse in the summer.
3 Do you like .... in the ocean?
4 We often go to clubs because we like
   ....
5 I sometimes go .... on the ice in the winter.
6 I don't like art because I don't like
   ....
7 You need a large, heavy ball for
   ....
8 In music class we can ....

★★ **6** Choose an activity and write your own short description. Use the models in Exercise 5.

Activity	Equipment	Place
surfing	surfboard	in the ocean
dancing	dancing shoes	in a theater
horseback riding	horse	in the mountains
painting	paint and paper	in the countryside

Vocabulary page 108

Reading

★ **1** Read the extract from a story. Match the people (1–5) to the activities (a–e).

1 Ross and Lizzy   a mountain biking
2 The birds   b hiking
3 A girl   c having a picnic
4 A man   d horseback riding
5 A family   e singing

Brain Trainer

Put new words in topic groups. This will help you learn them more easily and understand texts about a particular topic.

Look at the words and guess which word is not in the story.

adventure	horseback riding	mountains
hiking	river	swims
climb	bike	

Now read the text and check.

Ross and Lizzy are at an adventure camp. It's the first day of their vacation, and they are horseback riding in the mountains. It's a beautiful afternoon. The sun is shining, and the birds are singing. The horses aren't walking very fast. They can see some people. A girl is mountain biking, there's a man hiking with his dog, and a family is having a picnic next to the river. Suddenly, there's a loud noise. Someone is shouting for help. Ross and Lizzy get down from their horses and run to the river.

"Look! There's a boy in the water. He can't swim," says Lizzy.

Ross jumps into the river and swims to him.

Ross says to the boy, "It's OK. I can help you."

Ross and the boy climb out of the water onto the grass. The boy is safe, but he's crying.

"What's wrong?" asks Ross.

"My bike's in the river with my cell phone and keys."

The children look at the water.

"There it is," says the boy.

"What's that next to your bike?" asks Lizzy. "It isn't moving, and it's big. What is it?"

★★ **2** Read the extract again. Are the statements true (T) or false (F)?

1 Ross and Lizzy are on vacation.   *T*
2 The man has a dog with him.   ....
3 The horses run to the river.   ....
4 There's a girl in the water.   ....
5 Ross doesn't help the boy.   ....
6 The boy's bike is in the river.   ....

★★ **3** Read the extract again. Choose the correct options.

1 Ross and Lizzy *are* / *aren't* in the mountains.
2 The family *has* / *doesn't have* a dog.
3 Ross and Lizzy *hear* / *don't hear* a loud noise.
4 The boy *can* / *can't* swim.
5 Ross *jumps* / *doesn't jump* into the river.

★★ **4** Guess what's in the river next to the boy's bike. Then read and find out what it is.

1 a fish
2 a box full of money
3 an old statue
4 an old boat

"Look, Lizzy. It's the head of an old statue— the head of the statue in the town square."

"Why is it here?"

"I don't know. Let's call the adventure camp and tell them. They can help us get the bike out of the river, too."

Grammar • Present continuous

★ 1 Look at the picture. Complete the sentences with the Present continuous affirmative of these verbs.

| play | ~~rollerblade~~ | run | sing | walk | watch |

1 The girl *'s rollerblading* in the park.
2 The boy ....
3 The children .... in the playground.
4 Their grandparents .... them.
5 The woman .... with her dog.
6 The bird .... in the tree.

★ 2 Complete the sentences with the Present continuous negative of these verbs.

| dance | ~~have~~ | run | take |

At the camp …
1 The children *aren't having* lunch outside because the weather is bad.
2 He .... in the race because he can't find his sneakers.
3 They .... because there isn't any music.
4 I .... photos today because I don't have my camera.

★★ 3 Look at the pictures. Write sentences.

1 hike / bike
They *aren't hiking. They're biking.*
2 swim / surf
The man ....
3 dance / do gymnastics
My sister ....
4 take photos / paint
The children ....

★★ 4 Complete the text with the correct form of the verbs.

The camp is busy today. We ¹ *'re doing* (do) a lot of different activities. Some people ² .... (swim) in the lake. I ³ .... (not swim) because it's cold. I ⁴ .... (kayak) with Will and Beth. Our counselor, Mr. Carter, ⁵ .... (check) the boats, and he ⁶ .... (tell) us what to do. My brother and sister are in the mountains. They ⁷ .... (go) up Mount Peak today. They ⁸ .... (not walk); they ⁹ .... (bike) to the top.

• Present continuous: questions and short answers

★ 5 Complete the questions with *Am, Is* or *Are*.

1 *Are* you painting those flowers?
2 .... I playing tennis with you?
3 .... the cat climbing the tree?
4 .... Ben and Emma surfing?
5 .... the girl ice skating?

★ 6 Match the questions in Exercise 5 to the answers (a–e).

a No, it isn't. ☐   d Yes, you are. ☐
b No, I'm not. ☑   e Yes, they are. ☐
c Yes, she is. ☐

★★ 7 Look at the pictures. Complete the questions and answers.

1 *Is he skateboarding?* (skateboard)
No, he isn't.
2 .... ? (surf)
....
3 .... ? (bowl)
....
4 .... ? (run)
....

Grammar Reference pages 94–95

Vocabulary • Weather and seasons

★1 **Find the seasons. Then complete the sentences.**

1 The days are hot and sunny, and people go to the beach in *summer.*
2 It often snows in ....
3 In .... the plants grow, and the trees are in flower.
4 It's foggy and windy in ...., and the leaves on the trees turn brown.

★2 **Find and write the other words in Exercise 1.**

1 .... 2 .... 3 ....

★3 **Label the weather symbols.**

| cloudy | ~~foggy~~ | raining |
| snowing | sunny | windy |

1 *foggy* 2 ....

3 .... 4 ....

5 .... 6 ....

★★4 **Look at the pictures. Write the season and weather.**

1 *It's winter. It's cold, and it's snowing.*

2 ....

....
3 ....

4 ....

★★5 **Complete the sentences with your own ideas.**

1 In the fall the weather *is / isn't*

....

2 In summer I *go / don't go* to

....

3 I *like / don't like* winter because

....

4 In spring we *can / can't* (see)

....

5 My favorite season is

....

because ....

Vocabulary page 108

Chatroom Expressing surprise

Speaking and Listening

★ **1** Listen and complete the table.
18

Expresses surprise	Doesn't express surprise
1	

★ **2** Listen and read the conversation. Who is surprised,
19 Frank or Beth? Underline the expressions of surprise.

Beth Hi, Frank. I'm glad you're here. Do you have your camera with you?

Frank I have my cell phone. I can take photos with that. Why do you need a camera?

Beth Can you see those two people over there? They're playing tennis.

Frank Yes. Who are they?

Beth That's Brad Pitt and Anthony Mackie.

Frank Wow! How amazing! Why are they here?

Beth They're filming in a big house downtown.

Frank Really? That's cool.

Beth Let's take some photos.

Frank And look! There's Angelina Jolie as well! She's my favorite actor.

Beth We can ask for their autographs, too. This is so exciting!

★★ **3** Read the conversation in Exercise 2 again. Complete the sentences.

1 Beth asks Frank for a *camera*.
2 Frank has his .... with him.
3 Brad Pitt and Anthony Mackie are playing
....
4 Angelina Jolie is Frank's favorite
....
5 Frank and Beth want the actors' photos
and ....

★★ **4** Complete the conversations with these responses.

> How amazing! Can you talk to him?
> Look! There's a man juggling six balls!
> ~~Really? That's a lot of babies!~~
> Wow! That's awesome! Thank you so much.

1 Flies can have five trillion babies in one year!
Really? That's a lot of babies!
2 Guess what? I'm standing next to Leo Messi!
....
3 This is a great festival.
....
4 I have a surprise for you. Here are some tickets to Disneyland.
....

★★ **5** Complete the conversation with your ideas.

You	Hi, ¹ .... *(name)* How are you?
Your friend	I'm fine, thanks. Where are you?
You	I'm in ² .... *(place)*
Your friend	³ .... *(response)*. What are you doing there?
You	I'm on vacation with ⁴ .... *(friend or family member)*. We're ⁵ .... *(activity)*
Your friend	⁶ .... *(response)* Guess what I'm doing!
You	Are you ⁷ .... *(activity)*?
Your friend	No, I'm in ⁸ .... *(place)*, and I'm talking to ⁹ .... *(person)*
You	¹⁰ .... *(response)*

Speaking and Listening page 117

Grammar • Present simple and Present continuous

★ 1 Match each person to two sentences.

1 [c] [f] 2 [ ] [ ] 3 [ ] [ ]

 student    doctor    artist

4 [ ] [ ] 5 [ ] [ ] 6 [ ] [ ]

 radio DJ    actor    zookeeper

a I work in the hospital.
b I'm interviewing Katy Perry for today's show.
c I'm doing my homework now.
d I usually work in the theater.
e I paint pictures of people.
f I walk to school every morning.
g I'm making a movie in Hollywood at the moment.
h I always get up early to feed the animals.
i I'm cleaning out the animal enclosures now.
j I play songs on the radio every morning.
k I'm taking care of a sick baby.
l I'm drawing a girl at the moment.

★ 2 Write the sentences in Exercise 1 in the correct place.

1 Present simple: What do they usually do?
   1 *I walk to school every morning.*
   2 ....
   3 ....
   4 ....
   5 ....
   6 ....

2 Present continuous: What are they doing now?
   1 *I'm doing my homework now.*
   2 ....
   3 ....
   4 ....
   5 ....
   6 ....

Grammar Reference pages 94–95

★★ 3 Complete the description with the Present simple or Present continuous form of the verbs.

Ms. Sutton [1] *is* (be) a PE teacher. She [2] .... (work) at the middle school in Purcell. Every day she [3] .... (get up) early and [4] .... (bike) to school. Classes [5] .... (start) at 9 a.m. Today is Wednesday, and at the moment she [6] .... (teach) the first class. The students [7] .... (not play) soccer outside because it [8] .... (rain). They [9] .... (do) gymnastics indoors.

> **Brain Trainer**
>
> **Look for patterns in the language. Is the word order for questions the same in the Present simple and the Present continuous?**
>
> | Auxiliary verb | Subject | Main verb |
> |---|---|---|
> | *Are* | *you* | *studying English now?* |
> | *Do* | *you* | *have any pets?* |
>
> **Now do Exercise 4.**

★★★ 4 Write the questions and true answers.

1 you / study English / now?
   Are you studying English now?   *Yes, I am.*
2 it / rain / at the moment?
   ....
   ....
3 you / sometimes / get up early?
   ....
   ....
4 your family / usually / watch TV / in the evening?
   ....
   ....
5 you / go to the movies / on the weekend?
   ....
   ....
6 your teacher / give you homework / every week?
   ....
   ....

Reading

1 Read Holly's diary. Write the days under the correct weather.

1 .... 2 *Monday* 3 ....

4 .... 5 ....

Holly

Monday

My brothers and I are visiting my grandparents this week. They live in a small house in the country. They have some chickens and a pet goat. I love it here, but we can't see very much at the moment because it's foggy!

Tuesday

We get up early every day because there's a lot to do. In the mornings, Grandpa feeds the animals and cleans the enclosures. We help him. Today we're helping him in the yard. He's making a shed, but it isn't a good day to do this because it's very windy!

Wednesday

We're hiking today. It's cloudy, but it isn't cold. It's very good weather for walking! At the moment we're eating our lunch next to a lake. Grandma makes fantastic picnics!

Thursday

It's hot and sunny, and we're at the beach today. I'm sitting with Grandpa, and we're watching my brothers. They're surfing. It's difficult, and they aren't very good!

Friday

We're going home today, and Mom's coming to pick us up. We're waiting for her. It's raining, so we're watching TV.

2 Read Holly's diary again. Complete the sentences with the correct names.

Grandpa	Grandma	Her brothers
~~Holly~~	Mom	

1 *Holly* and her brothers are visiting their grandparents.

2 .... feeds the chickens and the goat every morning.

3 .... makes fantastic picnics.

4 .... can't surf very well.

5 .... is picking up Holly and her brothers.

3 Answer the questions.

1 What animals do Holly's grandparents have?
They have some chickens and a pet goat.

2 What is Grandpa making in the yard?
....

3 Do they get up early every day?
....

4 Where are they having lunch on Wednesday?
....

5 Who's sitting on the beach on Thursday?
....

6 Why are Holly and her brothers watching TV on Friday?
....

Listening

1 Listen and mark Julia and Dan's next subject.
20

1 English ☐   2 art ☐   3 PE ☐   4 science ☐

2 Listen again. Are the statements true (T) or false (F)?
20

1 Helen and George are playing tennis.   *T*
2 Julia and Dan can play golf or tennis.   ....
3 Julia doesn't have her swimsuit with her.   ....
4 Dan likes playing soccer in the rain.   ....
5 Julia goes ice skating every day in winter.   ....
6 Dan's favorite sport is surfing.   ....

Writing • A blog

1 **Put the words in the correct order.**

1 his blog / Paul / writing / is
Paul is writing his blog.

2 start / at one thirty / The races

....

3 doesn't / Newton / the team competition / win / usually

....

4 is / Paul / a red shirt / wearing / not

....

5 He / in the 100-meter race / is

....

2 **Read the blog. Are the statements in Exercise 1 true (T) or false (F)?**

1 *T*   2 ....   3 ....   4 ....   5 ....

← → C ⌂   ⊗

Thursday lunchtime

I'm really excited because it's Sports Day at school today. It's one thirty now, and the races start at two o'clock. At the moment, it's cloudy. This is good because it isn't very hot. There are six different teams. My team is called Newton, and our team color is yellow. The Watt team usually wins the team competition, but this year we want to win. I love running, and I'm in the 400-meter race. I'm also doing the high jump. My mom's coming to watch.

3 **Read the blog again. Complete the chart for Paul.**

		Paul	You
1	What day and time is Sports Day?	*Thursday 2 p.m.*	
2	What's the weather like?		
3	How many teams are there?		
4	What's your team?		
5	What do you wear?		
6	What events are you in?		

4 **Complete the chart in Exercise 3 for you.**

5 **Write a short blog about Sports Day at your school. Use the model in Exercise 2 and your notes from Exercise 4.**

....
....
....
....
....
....
....
....
....
....
....
....
....
....
....
....
....

6 Delicious!

Vocabulary • Food and drinks

★ (1) **Match the descriptions (1–6) to the food (a–f).**

1 I'm having a tuna sandwich and some juice.
  I have a banana, too.   *e*
2 I have a ham, cheese and tomato
  sandwich, and a glass of water.   ....
3 I'm eating rice with shrimp, and a yogurt.   ....
4 I want chicken with pasta and broccoli.   ....
5 I'm having fried sausage, eggs and bread.   ....
6 I want salmon, vegetables and a cup of tea.   ....

a Jake   b Florence   c Michael

d Anita   e Sally   f Nick

★ (2) **Look at the pictures in Exercise 1. Complete the sentences with these words.**

banana	bread	broccoli
ham, cheese and tomato sandwich		chicken
eggs	juice	pasta
~~rice~~	salmon	sausage
~~shrimp~~	tea	tuna sandwich
vegetables	water	~~yogurt~~

1 Jake is having *rice*, *shrimp* and a *yogurt*.
2 Florence is having .... , ...
  and ....
3 Michael is having .... , ...
  and ....
4 Anita is having .... , ...
  and ....
5 Sally is having a .... , a ....
  and some ....
6 Nick is having a .... and a glass of
  ....

★★ (3) **Match the sentence beginnings (1–6) to the endings (a–f).**

1 Bread and pasta are *e*
2 Chicken and sausage are
3 Salmon and tuna are
4 Tea and orange juice are
5 Bananas and carrots are
6 Cheese and yogurt are

a fruits and vegetables.
b fish.
c dairy products.
d meat.
e carbohydrates.
f drinks.

★★ (4) **Complete the text with these words.**

broccoli	carbohydrates	meat	pasta
salmon	~~vegetables~~	water	yogurt

Every day we eat a lot of different kinds of food.
It's good to eat a lot of fruits and [1] *vegetables*
like apples and [2] .... because they are
healthy foods. Milk, cheese and [3] ....
help your bones grow. It is important to eat
some [4] .... (like chicken), but don't
eat a lot of red meat. It is also good to eat
a lot of fish (like [5] ....). We need
[6] .... , so eat some bread,
[7] .... or rice with every meal. And
don't forget to drink a lot of [8] ....

★★★ (5) **Write five true sentences about your meals.**

1 For breakfast, I eat ....
2 For lunch, I usually have ....
3 For dinner, my family ....
4 My favorite food ....
5 My favorite drink ....
6 I don't like ....

Vocabulary page 109

Reading

★ **1** Read the article quickly. Write where the breakfasts come from.

China

....

cereal

....

★ **2** Read the article again. Write *Emily, Aga* or *Ming*.

1 *Aga*'s eating bread.
2 .... 's eating potatoes.
3 .... 's eating rice.
4 .... 's eating carrots.
5 .... 's eating ham.
6 .... 's eating bacon.

★★ **3** Read the article again. Correct the sentences.

1 Emily has a traditional breakfast every day.
   Emily has a traditional breakfast on Sundays.
2 On school days, Emily drinks a glass of orange juice.
   ....
3 Aga never has sausage for breakfast.
   ....
4 Aga's drinking a cup of tea today.
   ....
5 Ming never has a cooked breakfast.
   ....
6 Ming's favorite breakfast is rice with chicken.
   ....

★★ **4** Answer the questions.

1 What day does Emily say it is?
   She says it's Sunday.
2 Where are the potatoes?
   ....
3 Where can Emily buy more bread?
   ....
4 Where does Aga come from?
   ....
5 Who sometimes cooks breakfast for Aga?
   ....
6 What does Ming usually eat for breakfast?
   ....
7 Who is eating eggs today?
   ....

Breakfast Around the World

The first meal of the day is breakfast. Everyone eats breakfast, but people eat different food in different countries.

My name's Emily, and I'm American. It's Sunday, and we're having a traditional breakfast today. We have some bacon, eggs and cooked potatoes in the fridge. We don't have much bread for toast, but I can buy some more at the supermarket. We don't have a cooked breakfast every day. On school days, I have cereal and a glass of milk.

I'm Aga, and I come from Poland. My mom sometimes cooks me sausage for breakfast, but I usually have bread with some meat or cheese. Today I'm eating bread and ham because we don't have any cheese. I'm drinking a glass of orange juice, too.

My name's Ming, and I'm from China. My breakfast is always cooked. I usually have rice with fish or meat, and vegetables. My favorite breakfast is rice with shrimp, but we don't have any shrimp today. There isn't any chicken, either. There are a lot of vegetables, so I'm having rice with eggs, carrots and broccoli for breakfast this morning.

Grammar • Countable and uncountable nouns

★ 1 Write C (countable) or U (uncountable) next to each word.

1 tea   *U*   4 ham   ....
2 potato   ....   5 egg   ....
3 bread   ....   6 juice   ....

★ 2 Find the uncountable noun in each group.

1 eggs   (water)   tomatoes   vegetables
2 rice   bananas   sandwiches   potatoes
3 apple   orange   banana   pasta
4 music   song   guitar   MP3 player
5 comic   wallet   money   watch

★★ 3 How do you say these words? Write the words in the correct column. Then listen and check.
21

| banana | pasta | potato | salmon |
| sausage | water | yogurt | |

1 <u>chi</u>cken	2 to<u>ma</u>to

★★ 4 Complete the text with *a*, *an* or *some* and these words.

| apple | banana | ~~bread~~ |
| cheese | juice | tomatoes |

Sam and Ella are having a picnic today.

They have ¹ 🥖 *some bread* and

² 🧀 .... .They have

³ 🍅 .... , too. Sam has

⁴ 🍌 .... , and Ella has

⁵ 🍎 .... .They also have

⁶ 🧃 ....

• Many/Much/A lot of

★ 5 Complete the questions with *How many/much*.

1 *How much* bread is there?
2 .... cheese is there?
3 .... apples are there?
4 .... sandwiches are there?
5 .... water is there?
6 .... bananas are there?

★★ 6 Look at the pictures. Answer the questions in Exercise 5 with *Not much/many* or *A lot of*.

1 *A lot of bread*   2 ....   3 ....

4 ....   5 ....   6 ....

★★ 7 Look at the pictures and write what they have. Use *much/many* or *A lot of*.

1 books
She has a lot of books.

2 money
....
....

3 apples
....
....

4 DVDs
....
....

Grammar Reference pages 96–97

Vocabulary • Adjectives

★ **(1)** **Read the sentences and mark the correct pictures.**

1 Fido is a very quiet dog.
2 Our car is always clean. It's never dirty.
3 This cup of tea is cold.
4 This is a very large beach ball.
5 This is a horrible beach.
6 This apple is disgusting.

1 a ☑   b ☐   2 a ☐   b ☐

3 a ☐   b ☐   4 a ☐   b ☐

5 a ☐   b ☐   6 a ☐   b ☐

★ **(2)** **Find 12 adjectives. Then label the pictures in Exercise 1.**

N	O	I	S	Y	D	X	G	D	Q
K	H	O	R	R	I	B	L	E	D
W	O	N	D	E	R	F	U	L	W
B	T	G	R	G	T	A	I	I	L
N	R	D	S	E	Y	W	E	C	A
T	S	I	M	A	L	Q	Y	I	R
C	L	E	A	N	H	U	A	O	G
O	E	I	L	H	T	I	N	U	E
L	N	E	L	C	N	E	R	S	A
D	I	S	G	U	S	T	I	N	G

Picture 1   a *quiet*   b ....
Picture 2   a ....   b ....
Picture 3   a ....   b ....
Picture 4   a ....   b ....
Picture 5   a ....   b ....
Picture 6   a ....   b ....

★★ **(3)** **Put the letters in the correct order.**

1 It's a *hot* (oth) and sunny day.
2 I'm on the beach eating ....
   (uieidslco) ice cream.
3 We're staying in a .... (geral) hotel
   next to the beach.
4 There are a lot of .... (ysino) children
   playing with a beach ball.
5 The pool is .... (encal), and I go
   swimming every day.

★★ **(4)** **Write opposite sentences with these adjectives.**

cold	dirty	disgusting
horrible	quiet	~~small~~

1 My school is very large.
   My school is very small.
2 Our classroom's hot.
   ....
3 The food at school is delicious.
   ....
4 We're very noisy at lunchtime.
   ....
5 Dorothy is a wonderful singer.
   ....
6 The windows in our classroom are clean.
   ....

★★★ **(5)** **Write true sentences. Use these words and/or your own ideas.**

guitars	horse	mouse
tea	trumpets	water

1 noisy / quiet instruments
   Trumpets are noisy instruments. Guitars are quiet instruments.
2 delicious / disgusting food
   ....
3 a hot / cold drink
   ....
4 a wonderful / horrible TV show
   ....
5 a small / large animal
   ....
6 a clean / dirty job
   ....

Vocabulary page 109

Chatroom Ordering food

Speaking and Listening

★ **(1)** **Read the sentences. Write Waiter (W) or Customer (C).**

1 Are you ready to order? ___ W
2 I'd like a shrimp sandwich, please. ....
3 I'll have a tomato salad, please. ....
4 Would you like anything to drink? ....
5 Can I have ice cream, please? ....

★ **(2)** **Listen and read the conversation. Match the people to the food.**
22

1 Frank
2 Beth's mom
3 Beth

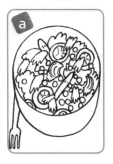 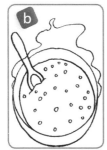 

Beth	I'm hungry.
Beth's mom	Me too! It's lunchtime. Let's go into this café.
Beth	Can we sit at the table next to the window? It's nicer than this one.
Beth's mom	I agree. It's quieter, too!
Waiter	Are you ready to order?
Beth's mom	Yes, we are. Frank, what would you like?
Frank	I'd like a ham and cheese sandwich, please.
Waiter	Would you like anything to drink?
Frank	A glass of orange juice, please.
Beth's mom	Beth?
Beth	A tuna salad for me, please. And orange juice too, please.
Waiter	Would you like some bread with that?
Beth	No, I'm OK, thanks.
Beth's mom	I'll have the soup, please. And can I have some water, please?
Waiter	Yes, of course.

★★ **(3)** **Read the conversation again. Are the statements true (T) or false (F)?**

1 Frank, Beth and her mom go to a restaurant. ___ F
2 They sit next to the window. ....
3 They order food for lunch. ....
4 Frank and Beth ask for smoothies. ....
5 Beth would like some bread. ....
6 Beth's mom would like some water. ....

★★ **(4)** **Complete the conversation. Then listen and check.**
23

| drink | have | ice cream | I'd | OK | ~~order~~ |

Waiter	Are you ready to ¹ *order*?
Customer	Yes. ² .... like a tuna salad, please.
Waiter	Would you like some bread?
Customer	No, I'm ³ .... , thanks.
Waiter	Would you like anything to ⁴ ....?
Customer	I'll ⁵ .... orange juice, please.
Waiter	Would you like anything else?
Customer	I'd like some ⁶ .... , please.
Waiter	Yes, of course.
Customer	Thank you.

★★ **(5)** **Look at the menu. Write a conversation between a waiter and a customer. Use the model in Exercise 4.**

● **Main course**
tuna salad   pasta with chicken
burger and fries   ham and cheese pizza

● **Drinks**
water   orange juice   smoothie

● **Desserts**
chocolate cake   ice cream   fruit salad

Speaking and Listening page 118

Grammar • Comparatives

★ 1 Write the comparative form of these adjectives in the correct column.

clean	delicious	~~dirty~~	disgusting
easy	funny	hot	~~interesting~~
large	~~nice~~	~~small~~	white

Short adjectives	Short adjectives ending in -e
¹ *smaller*, ² .... , ³	⁴ *nicer*, ⁵ .... , ⁶ ....
Adjectives ending in -y	**Long adjectives**
⁷ *dirtier*, ⁸ .... , ⁹	¹⁰ *more interesting*, ¹¹ .... , ¹² ....

★ 2 Complete the sentences with the comparative form of the adjectives.

1 The Station Hotel is *smaller* (small) than the Park Hotel.
2 This café is .... (noisy) than the restaurant.
3 The French menu is .... (difficult) to understand than the English menu.
4 The waiter is .... (young) than the customer.
5 Lunch is .... (cheap) than dinner.
6 These salads are .... (good) than the pizzas.

★★ 3 Rewrite the sentences in Exercise 2 with these adjectives.

| bad | easy | expensive | ~~large~~ | old | quiet |

1 The Park Hotel *is larger than* the Station Hotel.
2 The restaurant .... the café.
3 The English menu .... the French menu.
4 The customer .... the waiter.
5 Dinner .... lunch.
6 The pizzas .... these salads.

★★ 4 Complete the text with the comparative form of the adjectives.

My family isn't big. There's just my mom, my sister and me. I'm 13, and she's 11. My sister's ¹ *younger* (young) than me, but she's ² .... (tall). We live in a small apartment. I have a ³ .... (big) bedroom than she does, but her room is ⁴ .... (clean) and ⁵ .... (neat). At school, we like different subjects. I'm ⁶ .... (good) at English and French, but she finds languages ⁷ .... (difficult) than I do. She likes PE, and she's a fast runner. She's ⁸ .... (fast) than me. She has a lot of friends, and she's ⁹ .... (popular) than me! She's ¹⁰ .... (noisy), too!

★★★ 5 Compare these things. Use the adjectives.

1 red car (expensive)
   blue car (cheap)

2 green bag (small)
   yellow bag (large)

3 Sam's bike (new)
   Tom's bike (old)

4 June's phone (noisy)
   Ella's phone (quiet)

5 Sam's T-shirt (dirty)
   Dan's T-shirt (clean)

1 *The blue car is cheaper than the red car.*
  The red car is more expensive than the blue car.
2 ....
  ....
3 ....
  ....
4 ....
  ....
5 ....
  ....

Grammar Reference pages 96–97

Reading

1 Read the profile. Choose the correct sentence.

1 Jamie Oliver is a farmer.
2 Jamie Oliver is a TV chef.
3 Jamie Oliver is a school teacher.

> **Brain Trainer**
>
> **When you see a new word similar to a word you know, guess the meaning. Find *cooking* in the text. What do you think it means?**
>
> Verb   Noun
> *cook*   *a cook*
>
> **Now read the profile.**

Jamie Oliver is a busy man. What does he do? He's a chef, and he loves cooking. He has his own TV shows. He writes cookbooks. He has a website with a blog and a lot of ideas for things to cook. He gives cooking lessons. He has many restaurants.

Jamie wants everyone to eat and enjoy good food. Cooking is fun, and good food helps you live a long and happy life. He also works to help children and young people. His TV shows prove that food can be delicious *and* good for you.

Jamie cooks dishes from different countries on his TV shows. His *Jamie's Italian* restaurants serve food from Italy. His *Fifteen* restaurants are special. Some young people leave school and can't find work. Every year, fifteen of these young people start work in Jamie's restaurants and learn to cook. Some of them are now chefs and have their own restaurants.

2 Read the profile again. Are the statements true (T) or false (F)?

1 Jamie doesn't do very much.   F
2 He writes books about geography.   ....
3 He has a lot of restaurants.   ....
4 He wants people to eat well.   ....
5 He helps some young people without jobs. ....

3 Read the profile again. Answer the questions.

1 What is on Jamie's website?
   A blog and a lot of ideas for things to cook.
2 How does good food help you?
   ....
3 Which restaurants cook food from Italy?
   ....
4 How many young people start work at *Fifteen* every year?
   ....
5 Do some of these young people have their own restaurants now?
   ....

Listening

1 Listen and check the correct answer.

24   What is *Young Masterchef*?
   1 A TV cooking competition for children. ☐
   2 A restaurant in New York.   ☐
   3 A special school for chefs.   ☐

2 Listen again. Choose the correct answers.

24   1 George is …
      a this year's winner.   b last year's winner.
   2 He's …
      a 11 years old.   b 12 years old.
   3 George is cooking …
      a carrot soup.   b tomato soup.
   4 His favorite dish is …
      a strawberry ice cream.
      b strawberry cheesecake.
   5 George wants to have his own …
      a restaurant.   b TV show.

3 Listen again. Answer the questions.

24   1 How old are the children on *Young Masterchef*?
   ....
2 Who do the children cook for?
   ....
3 Is George cooking today?
   ....
4 What is George cooking with the fish?
   ....
5 What does George want to be?
   ....

Writing • Instructions

1 Number the sentences in order. Then rewrite them using *First, Then* and *Finally*.

toothpaste   toothbrush

1 ☐ Brush your teeth for two minutes.
  ☐ Rinse your brush and put it back in the cup.
  ☑ Put toothpaste and some water on your toothbrush.

1 *First, put toothpaste and some water on your toothbrush.*

2 ....
....

3 ....
....

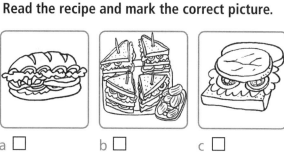

dog bowl   Dog   can

2 ☐ Give the bowl to the dog.
  ☐ Open a can of dog food.
  ☐ Put some food in the dog bowl.

....
....
....
....

2 Complete the instructions with these verbs.

add	blend	~~chop~~	enjoy	pour

1 *Chop* the banana.
2 .... some raspberries and yogurt.
3 .... the ingredients for a minute.
4 .... the mixture into a glass.
5 .... your smoothie with some friends.

3 Read the recipe and mark the correct picture.

a ☐   b ☐   c ☐

4 Read the recipe again. Answer the questions.

1 How many slices of bread are there?
....

2 Is there any mayonnaise on the bread?
....

3 What meat is in this sandwich?
....

4 What do you add first, the tomato or the chicken?
....

5 What do people often eat with the sandwich?
....

5 Now write a recipe for your favorite sandwich. Use *First, Then, Finally*. Use the recipe guide below, and the recipe in Exercise 3 to help you.

Make a .... sandwich
Ingredients
bread, ...
First, ...
....
....
....
....
....
....
....

Make a club sandwich

Ingredients

• three slices of white bread
• chicken
• tomato
• mayonnaise
• lettuce

First, toast the three slices of bread.
Then put mayonnaise on each slice.
Add the chicken to one slice of bread. Put another slice of bread on top of the chicken.
Put the tomato and lettuce on the second slice of bread. Put the last slice of bread on top.
Finally, cut the club sandwich into four pieces. Put it on a plate and enjoy it with some chips.

Check 2

Grammar

1 Write the rules. Use *You must* or *You mustn't*.

- tell someone where you are going ✓
- walk on your own ✗
- take food and water ✓
- go in foggy weather ✗
- take a map ✓

Rules for hiking in the mountains

0 *You must tell someone where you are going.*
1 ....
2 ....
3 ....
4 ....

/ 4 points

2 Complete the sentences with the Present simple or Present continuous.

0 We often *go* (go) to the zoo in the summer.
1 .... you .... (wear) your hat now?
2 Why .... they always ....
  (get up) early?
3 When .... he usually ....
  (finish) school?
4 .... she .... (do) gymnastics now?
5 We .... (not play) tennis on Sundays.
6 I .... (watch) a news show at the moment.

/ 6 points

3 Choose the correct options. Then complete the text with *much* or *many*.

How much food do we have? There ⁰(*isn't*)/
aren't much pasta, and there ¹ *isn't* / *aren't*
.... shrimp. There ² *isn't* / *aren't*
.... broccoli, and there ³ *isn't* / *aren't*
.... carrots. There ⁴ *is* / *are* a lot of eggs,
but there ⁵ *isn't* / *aren't* .... ice cream.

/ 5 points

4 Look at the pictures. Complete the sentences with these phrases. Then put the word in parentheses in the correct place.

go ice skating	~~go kayaking~~
go mountain biking	go rollerblading
go climbing	play the guitar

0 (often) He *often goes kayaking* when it's sunny.
1 (never) She ....
  when it's foggy.
2 (always) They ....
  when it's cloudy.
3 (usually) He ....
  when it's raining.
4 (hardly ever) He ....
  when it's windy.
5 (sometimes) They ....
  when it's cold.

/ 5 points

Vocabulary

5 Look at the pictures and complete the sentences.

0 The *spider* is smaller than the *hissing cockroach*.
1 The .... is larger than the ....
2 The .... is noisier than the ....
3 The .... is longer than the ....
4 The .... is smaller than the ....
5 The .... is dirtier than the ....

/ 5 points

6 **Label the pizzas.**

0 b*anana* pizza
1 c .... and h .... pizza
2 t .... and s .... pizza
3 c .... and t .... pizza
4 s .... and b .... pizza
5 s .... and e .... pizza

/ 5 points

Speaking

7 **Match the sentences (1–5) to the responses (a–e).**

0 I have the best grades in the class!   0
1 Do you like kayaking?
2 The football game isn't on TV today.
3 I have tickets for *X Factor* next week.
4 I can hear an insect. Can you see it?
5 I like dancing.

0 Wow! That's wonderful! Good job!
a How amazing! Lucky you!
b Me too! I love it.
c No. I don't like water sports.
d Yes. It's just a mosquito.
e Really? Oh! Why not?

/ 5 points

8 **Choose the correct options to complete the conversation.**

Waiter   Are you ready to order?
Mom   Yes, we are.
Waiter   What 0 *would you like* / *do you want*?
Sarah   1 *Give me* / *I'll have* the spaghetti, please.
Mom   And 2 *I'd like* / *I want* the burger with fries, please.
Waiter   3 *What do you want* / *Would you like anything* to drink?
Sarah   4 *Can I have* / *Give me* a glass of orange juice, please?
Mom   And 5 *I drink* / *I'd like* water, please.
Waiter   Yes, of course. Is that all?
Mom   Yes, thank you.

/ 5 points

Translation

9 **Translate the sentences.**

1 She hardly ever goes hiking in winter.
....
....
2 Are they feeding the rabbits?
....
....
3 How much bread do we have in the fridge?
....
....
4 Autumn is usually foggier than spring.
....
....
5 You must be quiet in the library.
....
....

/ 5 points

Dictation

10 **Listen and write.**
25

/ 5 points

Modern History

Vocabulary • Ordinal numbers, years, dates

★ **1** Find the ordinal numbers in the word snake. Then write them in the correct sentence.

seventhfourthfirstsixththirdsecondfifth

Dates the Harry Potter books go on sale:

1 1997   The *first* Harry Potter book.
2 1998   The .... book.
3 1999   The .... book.
4 2000   The .... book.
5 2003   The .... book.
6 2005   The .... book.
7 2007   The .... book.

★ **2** Choose the correct options.

1 May thirty-first
  May 13 / (*May 31*)
2 June ninth
  June 9 / June 19
3 July seventeenth
  July 17 / July 7
4 November twenty-second
  November 2 / November 22
5 March third, nineteen thirty-two
  March 3, 1932 / March 3, 1952
6 October fifteenth, two thousand ten
  October 13, 2001 / October 15, 2010

★★ **3** Complete the dates.

1 January first, two thousand
  January 1, *2000*
2 April second, nineteen sixty-six
  April ...., ...
3 February twenty-ninth, two thousand twelve
  February ...., ...
4 December tenth, nineteen eleven
  December ...., ...
5 September fourth, nineteen forty-four
  September ...., ...

★★ **4** Write the dates.

1 March third, nineteen thirty-two *3/3/1932*
2 September twenty-seventh, two thousand eleven   ....
3 February fourth, nineteen sixteen

  ....
4 October eighteenth, nineteen eighty-four

  ....
5 April twentieth, two thousand one

  ....
6 January thirteenth, nineteen fifty-seven

  ....

★★★ **5** Complete the sentences with the correct dates.

a   11/11/1918   b   8/4/2012   c   7/20/1969

d   5/6/1994   e   12/14/1911   f   3/9/1959

1 On *November eleventh, nineteen eighteen*, World War I ends.
2 On.. , Michael Phelps wins his eighteenth gold Olympic medal for swimming.
3 On .... , the first man walks on the moon.
4 On .... , the channel tunnel opens between France and England.
5 On .... , Roald Amundsen reaches the South Pole.
6 On .... , the Barbie doll goes on sale.

Vocabulary page 110

Reading

★ 1 **Read the text quickly. Mark the correct description.**

1 ☐ This is from Alice's letter.
2 ☐ This is from Alice's schoolbook.
3 ☐ This is from Alice's diary.

> **Brain Trainer**
>
> Look at the pictures. They often help you understand a text.
>
> Now do Exercise 2.

★ 2 **Read the text again. Number the pictures in order.**

a ☐

b ☐
underground tunnel

c ☐

d ☐

e ☐

★★ 3 **Read the text again. Match the sentence beginnings (1–6) to the endings (a–f).**

1 Tom likes
2 Alice is Tom's
3 Alice's diaries are
4 In 1940, Alice was
5 Alice's mom was
6 Alice's dad was

a grandmother.
b a good cook.
c 12 years old.
d family history.
e in France.
f from World War II.

★★★ 4 **Answer the questions.**

1 How many wartime diaries does Tom have?
He has seven diaries.

2 What is the date of the diary entry?
....

3 How many planes were over London on September 7?
....

4 Why were hundreds of people in the underground tunnel?
....

5 Why wasn't lunch nice?
....

6 Why is Alice's mom happy?
....

Alice

> *I like family history.*
> *We have the wartime diaries of my grandmother, Alice. There are seven diaries from 1939 to 1945, one for each year of World War II. This is an extract from her diary when she was twelve.*

Tom

London, September 8, 1940

Last night was scary. We were in the underground tunnel all night. They stop the trains when the planes come over so people can hide there. There were fifteen planes last night. There were hundreds of people with us. It was noisy, but we were safe. I was worried about our house, but it was still there in the morning!

Lunch wasn't very nice today. There wasn't any meat, and the vegetables were old. Mom's a good cook, but we can't buy much food. I can't remember the last time there were bananas in our house.

There's some good news. There was a letter from Daddy this afternoon. He was in France, but he's back in England now. He's fine, and he's coming home. Mom's very happy.

Grammar • Past simple: *to be*

★ 1 **Complete the sentences with *was/were*.**

1 They *were* in the supermarket an hour ago.
2 I .... at my grandparents' house last weekend.
3 Carol and Terry .... at the train station yesterday morning.
4 The juice .... in the fridge.
5 She .... in her room a minute ago.
6 We .... in Hawaii last summer.

★ 2 **Rewrite the sentences and questions for yesterday.**

Today	Yesterday
1 Are your friends at school?	*Were your friends at school?*
2 My mom isn't at work.	....
	....
3 Is your dad at home?	....
4 We aren't in the classroom.	....
	....
5 Is your favorite show on TV?	....
	....
6 I'm at the swimming pool.	....
	....
7 There isn't much food in the fridge.	....
	....
8 Are there any children in the park?	....
	....

★★ 3 **Look at the pictures. Complete the text with *was, were, wasn't* or *weren't*.**

Lizzie's blog:
I ¹ *was* busy on Saturday. In the morning my mom and I ² .... shopping downtown. We ³ .... there long because the weather ⁴ .... terrible. In the afternoon I ⁵ .... with my friends at the movies. We ⁶ .... happy because the movie ⁷ .... silly and boring. It ⁸ .... good. On Sunday I ⁹ .... at home with my family. We ¹⁰ .... in the backyard because it ¹¹ .... sunny.

• There was/There were

★ 4 **Choose the correct options.**

1 There (*wasn't*)/ *weren't* any music at the party.
2 There *was / were* a lot of cars outside the school last Saturday.
3 There *was / were* an interesting history class yesterday.
4 There *wasn't / weren't* any Internet or TV twenty years ago.

★★ 5 **Complete the questions with *Was/Were there … ?* Then write true answers.**

1 *Was there* any English homework last week?
Yes, there was. / No, there wasn't.
2 .... any snow last winter?
....
3 .... any good shows on TV last night?
....
4 .... many students in your class last year?
....
5 .... any rain yesterday?
....

★★★ 6 **Look at the pictures. Correct the sentences.**

1 There were some girls at the beach last summer.
There weren't any girls at the beach.
There were some boys.
2 There were some boys at the café yesterday.
....
3 There was a post office here two years ago.
....
4 There was a cat in the backyard ten minutes ago.
....

Grammar Reference pages 98–99

Vocabulary • Regular verbs

★ 1 Match the verbs (1–6) to the pictures (a–f).

1 call c   3 talk   5 work
2 answer   4 study   6 like

★ 2 Find the verbs.

~~ask~~   close   invent   listen   stop   travel

C	L	O	S	E	F	G
K	A	L	T	M	N	D
A	S	L	O	I	Z	O
B	K	A	P	N	I	U
X	T	R	A	V	E	L
L	I	S	T	E	N	P
W	R	T	C	N	L	S
G	R	E	W	T	O	E

★★ 3 Choose the correct pronunciation.
26 Then listen and check.

1 traveled	(/d/)	/ɪd/	/t/
2 stopped	/d/	/ɪd/	/t/
3 invented	/d/	/ɪd/	/t/
4 asked	/d/	/ɪd/	/t/
5 listened	/d/	/ɪd/	/t/
6 closed	/d/	/ɪd/	/t/

★★ 4 Complete the sentences with the words from Exercise 3.

1 John Logie Baird *invented* television.
2 I .... to the story on the radio yesterday.
3 They .... to Russia last year.
4 The stores .... at 8 p.m.
5 We .... a lot of questions.
6 The train .... at Edison Park station.

★★ 5 Match the verbs (1–6) to the phrases (a–f).

1 ask   a a window
2 listen   b to music
3 close   c to the US
4 call   d a question
5 travel   e in a school
6 work   f a friend

★★ 6 Complete the conversation with these words.

answer	asked	called	close	like
listen	stop	studying	talk	~~working~~

Elsa Where's mom?
Dad She's ¹ *working* at the hospital. Why?
Elsa A man ² .... and wanted to ³ .... to her.
Dad Who was it?
Elsa I don't know. I ⁴ .... him, but he didn't ⁵ ....
Colin Can you ⁶ .... the door, please? I'm doing my homework and I don't want to ⁷ .... to your conversation.
Elsa What are you ⁸ .... ?
Colin English.
Elsa Do you ⁹ .... English?
Colin Yes, I do. It's my favorite subject.
Dad Elsa, ¹⁰ .... talking to Colin and let him do his homework.
Elsa OK, Dad.

Vocabulary page 110

Speaking and Listening

Brain Trainer

Practice and learn the set phrases and expressions that make talking easier.
Read the conversation in Exercise 1 and find the phrases in the list.

Cool!	Great.	Hang on.
Here we are!	Hi, guys!	I know.
Let's go!	Me too!	See you later!
Yuck!	Yum!	Yes, of course.
What a pain!		

Now do Exercise 1.

★ **1** Listen and read the conversation. **Underline**
27 the past-time words and phrases.

Beth Hi, Frank!
Frank Hi! Where were you <u>last night</u>? I called, but you didn't answer!
Beth I was at the gym yesterday, and my phone wasn't on. Sorry. What are you doing here?
Frank There's a special showing of *ET* at the movie theater this afternoon. It was popular in the 1980s. I love it.
Beth Me too!
Frank I want to see it. Do you want to come, too?
Beth Yes, of course. I'd love to.
Frank Oh no!
Beth What is it?
Frank I got the time wrong. The movie started half an hour ago.
Beth And you got the day wrong. It was showing last week!
Frank What a pain! Let's watch a DVD at home instead.

★ **2** Read the conversation again. Correct the <u>underlined</u> time phrases.

1 Frank phoned Beth <u>this morning</u>.
  Frank phoned Beth last night.
2 *ET* was popular <u>in the 1960s</u>.
  ....
3 The movie started <u>two minutes ago</u>.
  ....
4 The movie was showing <u>yesterday</u>.
  ....

★★ **3** Complete the sentences.

afternoon	~~May~~	for an hour	two weeks

1 We moved last *May*.
2 I visited the doctor .... ago.
3 I waited at the station ....
4 They played basketball this ....

★★ **4** Match the questions (1–6) to the answers (a–f).
28 Then listen and check.

1 When was your last vacation?   c
2 Where were you last summer?
3 How long was the flight to Orlando?
4 How long was the vacation?
5 Who were you with?
6 What was your favorite day?

a I was there with my whole family.
b We were on the plane for two hours.
c It was in July, about eight months ago.
d I loved the day we were at Disney World.
e We were there for two weeks.
f We were in Orlando, Florida.

★★ **5** Write a conversation about your friend Amy's vacation. Use the information below.

Amy's summer vacation

When?	last August
Where?	to Costa Rica
How long the trip?	8 hours by plane
Who with?	my family
How long the vacation?	10 days
Favorite day?	the last day—we went snorkeling

Speaking and Listening page 119

Grammar • Past simple regular: affirmative and negative

★ 1 **Read the sentences and write *Past simple* or *Present simple*.**

1 I asked the teacher a question. *Past simple*
2 She doesn't watch TV in the morning.
....
3 We like going to the movies. ....
4 They didn't bike to school. ....
5 He studied Spanish and French. ....
6 You didn't call me. ....

★ 2 **Complete the table.**

Infinitive	Past simple affirmative	Past simple negative
1 answer	*answered*	*didn't answer*
2 travel	....	....
3 dance	....	....
4 jump	....	....
5 start	....	....
6 study	....	....

★★ 3 **Complete the sentences with the Past simple of the verbs.**

1 They *watched* (watch) an awesome movie.
2 You .... (not listen) to the teacher.
3 We .... (travel) for six hours.
4 He .... (not cook) dinner.
5 I .... (play) baseball with some friends.
6 She .... (visit) her grandmother.

★★ 4 **Look at the pictures. Complete the sentences with these phrases. Use the correct form of the Past simple.**

listen to jazz music	~~paint some fruit~~
play soccer	start a weather project
study plants	study the presidents

1 *In art, she painted some fruit.*
2 ....
3 ....
4 ....
5 ....
6 ....

Grammar Reference pages 98–99

★★ 5 **Look at the pictures. Write sentences about Donna when she was young. Use the Past simple form of these verbs.**

climb	listen	~~play~~	study
clean up	travel	watch	

1 *She didn't play tennis.*
2 ....
3 ....
4 ....
5 ....
6 ....
7 ....

art   PE   science

history   geography   music

Reading

1 Match the photos (1–3) to the headlines (a–c).

 Robber Escapes by Parachute

 On Top of the World

 THE FAIRY TALE WEDDING

2 Read the articles. Match the photos (1–3) and headlines (a–c) to the articles.

1 ..... . Photo ☐

On May 26, 1953, two of the British expedition climbed all day, but they didn't reach the top of the mountain. The next two days were cold and windy. On May 28, a group of men started the climb. ¹ .... At 11:30 the next morning, New Zealander Edmund Hillary, and Tenzing Norgay from Nepal, reached the top of Mount Everest. ² ....

2 ..... . Photo ☐

On November 24, 1971, a man boarded a plane from Portland to Seattle. ³ .... The man handed a note to the flight attendant. The note said, "I have a bomb in my bag. Give me $200,000 and some parachutes, and nobody gets hurt." The plane landed in Seattle, and the man received the money and the parachutes. Then he ordered the pilot to fly to Mexico, and later he jumped off the plane using his parachute. ⁴ ....

3 ..... . Photo ☐

On Friday, April 29, 2011, Prince William married Kate Middleton. He is the grandson of the queen of England. ⁵ .... It was a beautiful wedding. ⁶ .... Thousands of people traveled to London and waited in the streets to see them. Millions of people around the world watched the wedding on TV.

3 Read the articles again. Six sentences are missing. Write the sentence letter in the correct place.

a He was around 40 years old, and he looked like any other passenger.
b They studied together at St. Andrews University in Scotland.
c They camped on the mountain that night.
d There were hundreds of people in Westminster Abbey.
e They stayed only 15 minutes at the top.
f This was one of the most mysterious robberies in US history.

4 Answer the questions.

1 Were Hillary and Norgay British?
No, they weren't.
2 What date were Hillary and Norgay at the top of Mount Everest?
....
3 What did the man on the plane look like?
....
4 What did the man do with the parachute?
....
5 Where was the wedding?
....
6 How many people were in the streets?
....

Listening

1 Listen and circle the correct date.

29
1 January 1, 2000
2 September 11, 2001
3 November 4, 2008

2 Listen and answer the questions.

29
1 Where was Katy?
She was at home in Kansas City.
2 Who was Katy with?
....
3 How old was Katy?
....
4 Where was Toby?
....
5 Who was Toby with?
....
6 Where were the fireworks?
....

Writing • An essay

1 Rewrite the sentences with the correct punctuation: commas, periods, question marks or exclamation points.

1 Where does your family come from
Where does your family come from?

2 I was born on January 14 1999

....

3 My grandparents came from Lamia a small town in Greece

....

4 Were your parents in school together

....

5 My grandparents aunts uncles and cousins all lived in that house

....

....

2 Read the essay. Match the sentence beginnings (1–5) to the endings (a–e).

1 Bonnie   a come from Dallas.
2 Her mom   b live in Dublin.
3 Her dad   c was born in Tampa.
4 Her grandparents d didn't stay in Dallas.
5 Her aunt and uncle e left his country many years ago.

My family history

My name's Bonnie, and I was born in Tampa, a city in Florida. I still live in Tampa with my family, but my parents weren't born here.

My mom grew up in Dallas, Texas, but she moved when she got a job in Tampa. She met my dad at a party. My mother's parents were from Dallas, too. I think her family lived in Dallas for many years.

My dad's family is Irish. My dad left Ireland when he was 21 because there wasn't any work there. My aunt and uncle live in Dublin, but I don't know much about my Irish family.

3 Read the essay again. Correct the sentences.

1 Tampa is a city in Texas.
Tampa is a city in Florida.

2 Bonnie's parents were born in Tampa.

....

....

3 Her mom moved to Ireland.

....

....

4 Her parents met at work.

....

....

5 Her mom's family comes from the country.

....

....

6 Her dad's family is Portuguese.

....

....

4 Answer the questions and take notes about your family.

Paragraph 1   Me
• Where were you born?
• Where do you live now?

Paragraph 2   My mom and her family
• Where is your mom from?
• Was her family from this place?

Paragraph 3   My dad and his family
• Where was your dad born?
• Was his family from this place?

5 Now write an essay about your family history. Use the model in Exercise 2 and your notes from Exercise 4 to help you.

....
....
....
....
....
....
....
....
....
....
....
....

Travel

Vocabulary • Means of transportation

★ **1** **Label the pictures.**

bike	bus	car	scooter	~~train~~	subway

1 *train*   2 ....   3 ....

4 ....   5 ....   6 ....

★ **2** **Complete the crossword.**

boat	bus	canoe	~~helicopter~~
truck	motorcycle	plane	

Across

3 **4** **5** **7**

Down

1 **2** **6**

★★ **3** **Complete the transportation groups.**

Name two types of …

1 water transportation   *boat*   ....
2 motor transportation you can ride

....

3 air transportation

....

4 rail transportation that carries a lot of people

....

5 road transportation you can drive

....

★★ **4** **Complete the sentences with these verbs.**

~~drives~~	flies	ride	sails	takes

1 My mom *drives* her car to work every day.
2 I .... my bike to school in the morning.
3 Susie often .... the bus downtown.
4 In the summer my dad .... his boat around the Caribbean.
5 The police officer .... the helicopter in case of an accident.

★★★ **5** **Read the text. Choose the correct options.**

In my family we all travel to school or work in different ways. My mom drives to work in her ¹ *car*. My dad has a ² .... because he transports fruits and vegetables to his store. My older sister rides her ³ .... to the airport. She flies small ⁴ .... to and from different places in the state. My brother is 16, and he rides a ⁵ .... to school. He wants a ⁶ .... when he is 17 because it's faster. My friends and I go to school on the school ⁷ .... There's a stop near my house.

1 a helicopter   b boat   **c** car
2 a van   b subway   c train
3 a bike   b boat   c canoe
4 a trains   b planes   c subway
5 a truck   b canoe   c scooter
6 a bike   b motorcycle   c truck
7 a bus   b van   c boat

Vocabulary page 111

Reading

★① **Read the websites. Match the photos (a–c) to the paragraphs (1–3).**

★② **Read the websites again. Write *Mark*, *Charlie* or *Sarah*.**

1 *Charlie* is American.
2 .... is Scottish.
3 .... is English.
4 .... started when he/she was 4 years old.
5 .... started when he/she was 10.
6 .... started when he/she was 12.

★★③ **Read the websites again. Are the statements true (T) or false (F)?**

1 Mark biked around the world when he was 15. *F*
2 Mark's video diary was for TV. ....
3 Charlie has flying lessons with his dad. ....
4 Charlie started flying in 2008. ....
5 Sarah was 17 in 2009. ....
6 Sarah was the first girl to win the Ginetta Junior Championship. ....

★★★④ **Answer the questions.**

1 Where did Mark bike in 1998?
 He biked from John O'Groats to Land's End.
2 How long was Mark's trip around the world?
 ....
3 Where were Charlie's flying lessons?
 ....
4 At what age can Charlie fly solo?
 ....
5 At what age can you drive in the UK?
 ....
6 What does Sarah want to do?
 ....

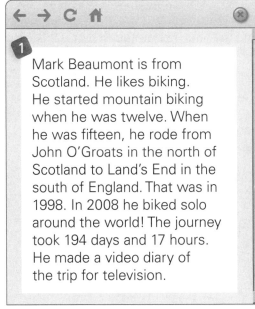

2

Charlie Goldfarb enjoys flying planes. In the summer of 2008, Charlie's father arranged some flying lessons for him near his home in California in the US, and he loved it. He was only ten years old. He is very good, but he can't fly solo until he is sixteen years old.

1

Mark Beaumont is from Scotland. He likes biking. He started mountain biking when he was twelve. When he was fifteen, he rode from John O'Groats in the north of Scotland to Land's End in the south of England. That was in 1998. In 2008 he biked solo around the world! The journey took 194 days and 17 hours. He made a video diary of the trip for television.

3

In the UK you can't drive on the street until you are 17 years old. However, Sarah Moore started driving on an airfield in England when she was four years old. In 2009 she won the Ginetta Junior Championship when she was 14. There aren't many female racing drivers, and Sarah was the first girl to win the championship. Her dream is to be the winner of the Le Mans car race.

Grammar • Past simple irregular: affirmative and negative

Brain Trainer

There are many irregular Past simple verbs. Do not try to learn them all at once. Learn three or four every day.

Now do Exercise 1.

★ 1 Write the verbs in the Past simple.

1 go   *went*
2 think   ....
3 take   ....
4 get   ....
5 buy   ....
6 understand   ....
7 have   ....
8 do   ....

★ 2 Complete the sentences with the negative form of the Past simple.

1 You *didn't understand* (understand) the question.
2 She .... (go) shopping.
3 I .... (ride) my scooter.
4 They .... (eat) breakfast.
5 He .... (drive) the car.
6 We .... (do) our homework.

★★ 3 Complete the sentences with the correct form of the verbs.

1 I *buy* flowers every week. Last week I *bought* some roses. (buy)
2 He usually .... the bus to work, but last week he .... the train. (take)
3 Last summer we .... to Spain by boat. We .... there every year. (go)
4 They always .... chicken for lunch on Sundays, but they .... fish today. (have)
5 She .... Tony on his bike this morning, but she usually .... him in the evenings. (see)
6 I usually .... milk for breakfast, but when we were on vacation, I .... orange juice. (drink)

Grammar Reference pages 100–101

★★ 4 Rewrite the sentences. Use the Past simple negative.

1 I did all my homework this week.
  I didn't do all my homework this week.
2 They bought an old white van.
  ....
3 My dad gave me five dollars.
  ....
4 I thought about our visit to Philadelphia.
  ....
5 She ate pizza for lunch.
  ....

★★ 5 Write Past simple sentences.

1 we / go / to the movies yesterday
  We went to the movies yesterday.
2 I / meet / my friend at the bus stop
  ....
3 my friend / give / me her old magazine
  ....
4 Mom / buy / a new camera
  ....
5 Dad / get / a new bike last week
  ....
6 they / have / lunch in a café
  ....

★★ 6 Complete the text with the Past simple form of the verbs.

Last weekend we visited an old mansion. My dad
[1] *drove* (drive), and the trip [2] .... (take) an hour and a half. We [3] .... (not get) there until ten thirty. We [4] .... (spend) the morning in the gardens. My brother [5] .... (see) a beautiful yellow bird, but I [6] .... (not see) it. There [7] .... (be) a café, but we [8] .... (not have) lunch there. We [9] .... (have) a picnic in the gardens. In the afternoon, we [10] .... (go) into the mansion. There [11] .... (be) a lot of rooms to see. I [12] .... (not like) the bathrooms, but I [13] .... (think) the kitchens were interesting. At the end of the day, I [14] .... (buy) a small key ring from the souvenir shop. We [15] .... (have) a wonderful day.

Vocabulary • Clothes

★ **1** Label the clothes.

| hat | pajamas | pants | scarf |
| shoes | skirt | ~~sneakers~~ | |

1 *sneakers*　　2 ....　　3 ....

4 ....　　5 ....

6 ....　　7 ....

★ **2** Match the descriptions (1–4) to the people (a–d).

Robin　Carly　Alexa　Sam

1 We're in the mountains in Vermont. It's cold, and I'm wearing a coat and boots.　*c Carly*
2 I'm camping with my family near the beach. I'm wearing shorts and a T-shirt.　.................
3 It's autumn, and it isn't very warm. I'm wearing jeans and a sweater.　.................
4 I'm on vacation in Miami. It's hot, and I'm wearing a dress and sandals.　.................

★★ **3** Look at the pictures in Exercise 2. Complete the descriptions.

| boots | coat | ~~dress~~ | jeans |
| sandals | shorts | sweater | T-shirt |

1 Alexa is wearing a *dress* and ....
2 Robin is wearing .... and a ....
3 Carly is wearing a .... and ....
4 Sam is wearing .... and a ....

★★ **4** Write the correct words. Then add your own ideas.

| coat | jeans | pajamas | shoes | ~~shorts~~ | skirt |

1 You wear these in summer.
   shorts　........................
2 You put this on to go outside in winter.
   ....　........................
3 You wear these on your feet.
   ....　........................
4 Boys don't wear this.
   ....　........................
5 You wear these on your legs.
   ....　........................
6 Something you wear in bed.
   ....　........................

★★ **5** Write true answers.

1 What are you wearing today?
   ....
2 What do you usually wear to school?
   ....
3 What do you wear at the beach?
   ....
4 What do you wear at night?
   ....
5 What do you wear on your feet?
   ....
6 What clothes do you have for parties?
   ....
7 What are your favorite clothes?
   ....

Vocabulary page 111

Chatroom Talking on the phone

Speaking and Listening

★ **1** Match the sentence beginnings (1–6) to the
30 endings (a–f) to make phrases for talking on
the phone. Then listen and check.

1 This	a on.
2 Is	b here he is.
3 Who's	c is Beth.
4 Hold	d this Frank?
5 Can I speak	e this?
6 Just a minute …	f to Frank, please?

★ **2** Listen and read the conversation. <u>Underline</u>
31 phrases from Exercise 1. Which phrases in
Exercise 1 are not in the conversation?

Frank's dad	Hello.
Beth	Hi. This is Beth. Is this Frank?
Frank's dad	Hello, Beth. No, it's Frank's dad.
Beth	Hello. Can I speak to Frank, please?
Frank's dad	Yes, of course. Frank! Just a minute … here he is.
Frank	Hi, Beth.
Beth	Hi, Frank. Listen, I had a piano lesson today, so I missed geography. Do we have any homework?
Frank	No, we don't, but Miss Woods gave us our books back. I have your homework book. I can bring it over to your house now.
Beth	That would be great! Thanks.
Frank	See you in a minute. Bye.
Beth	Bye.

★★ **3** Read the conversation again. Answer
the questions.

1 Who makes the phone call?
Beth makes the phone call.

2 Who answers the phone?
....

3 Who does Beth want to speak to?
....

4 Why wasn't Beth in geography class?
....

5 Why does Frank have Beth's homework book?
....

6 Where does Frank go at the end of
the conversation?
....

★★ **4** Complete the conversation with these words.
32 Then listen and check.

fine ~~Owen~~ Sally swimming pool two o'clock

Girl	Hello. Can I speak to ¹ *Owen*, please?
Boy	Hi, this is Owen. Is this Lettie?
Girl	No, it's ² ....
Boy	Oh. Hi, Sally. How are you?
Girl	I'm ³ .... , thanks. I'm going to the ⁴ .... this afternoon. Do you want to come, too?
Boy	Yes, I'd love to. What time are you going?
Girl	Let's meet there at ⁵ ....
Boy	Great! See you later.
Girl	Bye.

★★ **5** Write a phone conversation between you and
★ a friend. Use your own names, place and time
and/or the ideas below.

• Bert / Maggie / movie theater / five thirty
• Ali / Josh / library / 1:30
• Nicky / John / park / three fifteen
• Sarah / Faith / mall / one forty

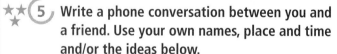

Speaking and Listening page 120

Grammar • Past simple: questions

★ 1 Read the questions and complete the answers.

1 Did you go to Lily's birthday party?
Yes, *I did.*

2 Did Lily have a birthday cake?
Yes, ...

3 Did Tom bring Lily a present?
Yes, ...

4 Did Lily's mom and dad dance?
No, ...

5 Did it rain?
No, ...

6 Did you and your friends enjoy the party?
Yes, ...

★ 2 Complete the questions.

Ryan Where ¹ *did* you *go* (go) yesterday?
Alice I went to the movies.
Ryan Who ² .... you .... (go) with?
Alice I went with my sister and two friends.
Ryan What ³ .... you .... (see)?
Alice We saw the last Harry Potter movie.
Ryan ⁴ .... you .... (enjoy) it?
Alice Yes. It was great!
Ryan What time ⁵ .... it .... (end)?
Alice It ended at ten o'clock.
Ryan How ⁶ .... you ....
(get) home?
Alice My mom picked us up and took us home.

★★ 3 Write the questions for the answers with these question words.

How	What	When	Where	Who	~~Why~~

1 *Why did you leave?*
I left because I was cold.

2 ....
He met Lucy and Mark.

3 ....
They arrived at six thirty.

4 ....
She wore a blue coat and a purple scarf.

5 ....
I went to the supermarket.

6 ....
We traveled by bus.

Grammar Reference pages 100–101

★★ 4 Look at the card. Write the questions about the missing information.

> Hi Louise,
> I'm on vacation in Spain with my family. We arrived here last ¹ ●. On Monday we went to the ² ●. I loved it. We ate ³ ● in an Italian restaurant in the evening. The next day we traveled by ⁴ ● to Cordoba. I saw ⁵ ● at the station! It's a small world! Enjoy your trip to Canada.
> Love, Ben

1 When *did Ben and his family arrive in Spain?*
2 Where .... ?
3 What .... ?
4 How .... ?
5 Who .... ?

★★ 5 Match the questions in Exercise 4 to the answers.

a ☐ He saw his Spanish teacher.
b ☐ They traveled by train.
c ☑ They arrived last night.
d ☐ They went to the theater.
e ☐ They ate pasta and shrimp.

★★ 6 Look at the picture of Jane's shopping trip last week. Write questions and answers.

1 where / go → downtown
Where did Jane go? She went downtown.

2 wear / hat / → yes
Did she wear a hat?
....

3 what / buy / → clothes
....
....

4 rain / → no
....
....

Reading

1 Read the quiz quickly. What means of transportation can you find?

boat, train, ...

2 Take the quiz. Then listen and check your answers.
33

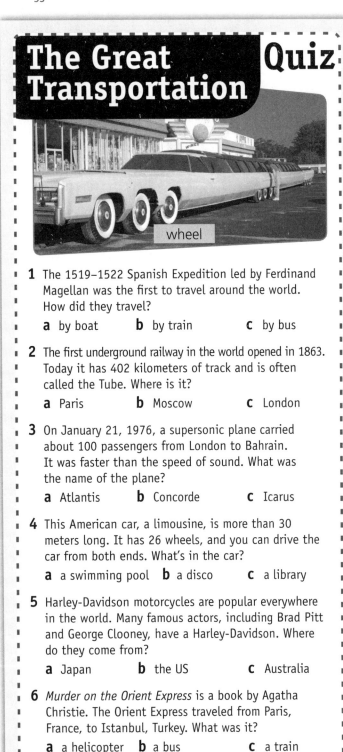

The Great Transportation Quiz

wheel

1 The 1519–1522 Spanish Expedition led by Ferdinand Magellan was the first to travel around the world. How did they travel?

a by boat   **b** by train   **c** by bus

2 The first underground railway in the world opened in 1863. Today it has 402 kilometers of track and is often called the Tube. Where is it?

a Paris   **b** Moscow   **c** London

3 On January 21, 1976, a supersonic plane carried about 100 passengers from London to Bahrain. It was faster than the speed of sound. What was the name of the plane?

a Atlantis   **b** Concorde   **c** Icarus

4 This American car, a limousine, is more than 30 meters long. It has 26 wheels, and you can drive the car from both ends. What's in the car?

a a swimming pool   **b** a disco   **c** a library

5 Harley-Davidson motorcycles are popular everywhere in the world. Many famous actors, including Brad Pitt and George Clooney, have a Harley-Davidson. Where do they come from?

a Japan   **b** the US   **c** Australia

6 *Murder on the Orient Express* is a book by Agatha Christie. The Orient Express traveled from Paris, France, to Istanbul, Turkey. What was it?

a a helicopter   **b** a bus   **c** a train

---

3 Now read about your score.

> **Your score?**
> 0–2 Oh no! Find out about transportation.
> 3–4 Great! You know some interesting facts.
> 5–6 Awesome!

4 Read the quiz again. Answer the questions.

1 Where did the first expedition to travel around the world come from? *It came from Spain.*

2 When did the Tube open?

....

3 Where did the supersonic plane fly on January 21, 1976?

....

4 How long is the limousine?

....

5 What is a Harley-Davidson?

....

6 Where did the Orient Express begin and end its trip?

....

Listening

1 Listen. Mark what the family is talking about.
34
1 Going on vacation.   ☐
2 Watching TV shows.   ☐
3 Buying a new car.   ☐

2 Listen again. Are the statements true (T) or false (F)?
34
1 They want to go to Oregon.   *T*
2 They live near Oregon.   ....
3 Sally takes a lot of books on vacation..   ....
4 Paul doesn't want to go by bus.   ....
5 They are talking about a winter vacation.   ....

3 Listen again. Answer the questions.
34
1 Why don't they go by plane? *It's expensive.*
2 Why don't they go by car?

....

3 Why don't they go by train?

....

4 Why don't they go by bus?

....

5 What does Mom suggest they do?

....

Writing • A travel diary

1 Read Karen's diary. Mark the correct statement (the paragraphs are not in order).

1 The paragraphs describe different sports. ☐
2 The paragraphs describe different times of the day. ☐
3 The paragraphs describe different places. ☐

a This evening we watched a funny movie in the theater. I'm writing this in bed. I'm sharing a bedroom with Patsy and Rosa. I must go to sleep now because there are a lot of activities tomorrow. I'm really excited because they look super fun!

b Today was the first day of our school trip to the Lakeside Adventure Center. The bus left from the school parking lot at eight thirty this morning. I sat next to Rosa. First, we ate the sandwiches from our packed lunch. Later we talked to the boys in the seat behind us. Then we ate everything else in our packed lunches. At twelve thirty the bus stopped for lunch, but we didn't have anything left!

c We arrived at two thirty. In the afternoon, we walked around the lake. Later we had dinner in the big hall.

2 Read the diary again. Number the paragraphs in order.

1 ....   2 ....   3 ....

3 Read the diary again. Answer the questions.

1 Where is the trip to?
   The trip is to the Lakeside Adventure Center.
2 When did the trip start?
   ....
3 How did they travel?
   ....
4 What did they do in the afternoon?
   ....
5 What did they do in the evening?
   ....
6 Who is sleeping in the same room as Karen?
   ....

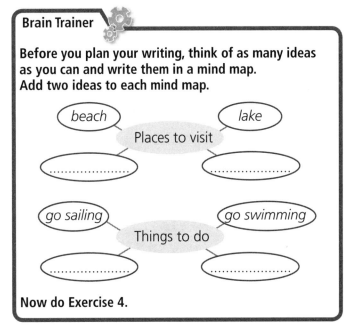

Brain Trainer

Before you plan your writing, think of as many ideas as you can and write them in a mind map.
Add two ideas to each mind map.

beach — Places to visit — lake
.... — ....

go sailing — Things to do — go swimming
.... — ....

Now do Exercise 4.

4 Take notes about your own school trip. Use the questions in Exercise 3.

Paragraph 1
1 ....
2 ....
3 ....

Paragraph 2
4 ....
5 ....

Paragraph 3
6 ....
7 ....

5 Write a short diary about the first day of your school trip. Use the model in Exercise 1 and your notes from Exercise 4.

....
....
....
....
....
....
....
....
....
....
....
....
....
....
....

Technology Time

Vocabulary • Technology

★ **1** Choose seven items of technology that you can touch.

broadband   social networking sites

Wi-Fi

blog

netbook

screen

smart phone

flash drive   instant messaging

digital radio

e-reader

interactive whiteboard

★ **2** Write the words from Exercise 1 next to the correct object.

1 *digital radio*   2 ....   3 ....

4 ....   5 ....

6 ....   7 ....

★ **3** Complete the conversation. Use the words you didn't choose in Exercise 1.

Dad   What are you doing?

Sarah   I'm trying to find Justin Bieber's ¹ *blog*. I want to know everything he does. The computer's really slow today. Why don't we have ² .... ?

Dad   We're getting it on Saturday. We're getting ³ .... too, so you can use your laptop in every room in the house.

Dad   I thought you were on Justin's website.

Sarah   No. I'm chatting with friends now.

Dad   You spend too much time on ⁴ ....

Sarah   I love them. The ⁵ .... is awesome. I can talk to all my friends at the same time.

Dad   You spend all day with your friends at school.

Sarah   But Dad, that's different!

★★ **4** Choose the correct options.

1 You want to read a novel. You can use …
   a instant messaging   b a digital radio
   c an e-reader

2 You want to talk to your friends. You can use …
   a instant messaging   b a flash drive
   c an interactive whiteboard

3 You want to take the homework you did on your computer to school. You can use …
   a Wi-Fi   b a screen   c a flash drive

4 You want to take a photo of your friends. You can use …
   a an e-reader   b a smart phone   c a blog

5 You want to listen to music. You can use …
   a a social networking site
   b a digital radio   c a screen

6 You want to write and tell people about what happens at school. You can use …
   a a blog   b broadband   c an e-reader

★★★ **5** Answer the questions.

1 What technology do you use at home?
....

2 What technology do you use at your school?
....

3 Who do you know that writes a blog?
....

4 What social networking sites do you use?
....

5 What can you do with a smart phone?
....

Vocabulary page 112

Reading ♪

★ **1** Read the advertisements quickly. Match the names (1–3) to the technology words (a–c).

1 The Candy 3G is
2 The Sung S2 is
3 The Albert 35 is

a a digital radio.
b an e-reader.
c a netbook.

★ **2** Read the advertisements again. Label the photos.

1 ....

2 ....

3 ....

★★ **3** Look at the advertisements again. Write Candy 3G (C), Sung S2 (S) or Albert 35 (A).

1 It has Wi-Fi.   S
2 You can choose its color.   ....
3 You can read novels on it.   ....
4 It's cheaper than the digital radio.   ....
5 You can watch movies on it.   ....
6 It doesn't have a screen.   ....

★★ **4** Answer the questions.

1 How many books can you store on the Candy 3G?

....

2 How much is the Candy?

....

3 How big is the netbook screen?

....

4 How much is the Sung S2?

....

5 Where is the best place for the digital radio?

....

6 How many colors can you choose from?

....

1

Sam's going to take her new Candy 3G on vacation. Why?

I want to go to the beach and read every day, but I don't want to take a lot of books. I'm going to take my Candy 3G because it's light, and I can carry it in my bag. It has all the books I want to read on it.

In fact, it stores up to 3,500 books, and it's only $150!

2

Buy the Sung S2, and you're going to love it! It's light, it's fast, and it's easy to use—and it has a 25 cm screen! You get Wi-Fi too, so you can go online wherever you are. Find your favorite websites. Enjoy chatting with friends. Watch movies and TV shows. Send emails. Play games. At $400, it's a winner!

3

The Albert 35 is just what you need next to your bed. Set your alarm for the morning, and you can wake up to your favorite music. And with the Albert 35, you can listen to your favorite shows at any time. It's also a CD player, and it can play from an MP3 player or a flash drive. It's available in red, black or white and costs $349!

Grammar • Be going to

★ 1 Choose the correct options.

1 They *isn't / aren't* going to work this evening.
2 *I'm going to / I'm going* take the bus.
3 Is he *go to / going to* close the door?
   Yes, *he is going to / he is.*
4 *Are you / Is you* going to listen to your new CD?
   No, *I'm not / I'm not going.*
5 *It not / It isn't* going to rain.
6 *We going to calling / We're going to call*
   our cousins.

★ 2 Complete the sentences with the correct form of *be going to* and the verb.

1 They *'re going to watch* (watch) a DVD tonight.
2 I .... (buy) a smart phone
   next month.
3 He .... (wear) his new
   shoes tomorrow.
4 She .... (not play) the guitar.
5 They .... (not go) bowling.
6 We .... (visit) the technology
   fair next week.

★★ 3 Look at the picture. Complete the sentences with *is/isn't/are/aren't going to* and the correct verb.

| buy | ~~meet~~ | play | stop | wear |

1 The girls *are going to meet* their friend.
2 The bus ....
3 The children .... tennis.
4 The man .... a newspaper.
5 The police officer .... his cap.

★★ 4 Look at the picture in Exercise 3. Complete the questions with *Is* or *Are*. Then answer the questions.

1 *Are* the girls going to go into the café?
   Yes, they are.
2 .... the woman going to get on the bus?
   ....
3 .... the children going to cross the street?
   ....
4 .... the man going to walk home?
   ....
5 .... the police officer going to drive the car?
   ....
6 .... it going to rain?
   ....

★★★ 5 What are you going to do this evening? Mark (✓ or ✗) the activities. Then write true sentences.

> My plans for this evening
> 1 do my homework
> 2 have dinner with my family
> 3 clean up my room
> 4 watch TV
> 5 go on a social networking site
> 6 go to bed early

1 *I'm going to do my homework./I'm not going to do my homework.*
2 ....
3 ....
4 ....
5 ....
6 ....

Grammar Reference pages 102–103

Vocabulary • Technology phrases

★ **1** Choose the correct options.

1 use the (Internet) / interactive
2 charge a search engine / a phone
3 download a phone / videos and movies
4 write a blog / Wi-Fi
5 go movies / online
6 send emails / online
7 use a text / Wi-Fi

★ **2** Put the letters in the correct order.

1 esdn a xtte   *send a text*
2 ues a erscha genein   ....
3 acth nloien   ....
4 rhaecg a npohe   ....
5 riewt a olbg   ....
6 londowad umics   ....

★★ **3** Look at the pictures. Complete the sentences with these phrases.

charging a phone	chatting online
~~downloading music~~	sending a text
writing a blog	

1 She's *downloading music.*
2 He's ....
3 He's ....
4 He's ....
5 She's ....

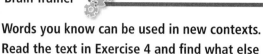

Brain Trainer

Words you know can be used in new contexts.
Read the text in Exercise 4 and find what else
you can download.
download music/movies/videos/ ...
Now do Exercise 4.

★★ **4** Choose the correct options.

We love technology in my family. My dad works
from home, so we have ¹ (Wi-Fi) / flash drive and
a super fast ² broadband / text connection. My
older sister ³ sends / goes online when she gets
home from school. She likes ⁴ chatting / using
with her friends online. My mom has a new
⁵ smart phone / instant messaging. She ⁶ writes /
uses it all the time. She likes it because it does
a lot of things. She can call people and take
photos, and she can ⁷ download / know her
emails wherever she is. Actually, she isn't using
it at the moment because it needs ⁸ emailing /
charging.

★★ **5** Complete the sentences with these words.
Then match the descriptions to the technology
(a–e) below.

| charge | chat | downloading | send | ~~use~~ |

1 Teachers *use* this in the classroom.   *b*
2 You must .... this before you take
  it to the beach to read your new book.   ....
3 You can call your friends, take photos and
  .... texts and emails with this.   ....
4 I'm .... the new movie so I can
  watch it tonight. Then I'm going to write
  about it tomorrow.   ....
5 You can .... online with your
  friends when you join this.   ....

a blog
b interactive whiteboard
c social networking site
d smart phone
e e-reader

Vocabulary page 112

Chatroom Asking for information

Speaking and Listening

★ **1** Match the statements (1–4) to the sentences asking for more information (a–d).

1 I missed math this morning.   *b*
2 There's a movie on tonight.
  Do you want to watch it?   ....
3 I'm having a bad day.   ....
4 I'm leaving school in July.   ....

a Why? Tell me about it.
b Why? What happened?
c Oh. What are you planning?
d What is it about? Can you tell me more?

★ **2** Listen and read the conversation. <u>Underline</u>
35 the phrases asking for information.

Frank	Beth, I'm writing about school clubs for the school newsletter. <u>Can you tell me about</u> the drama club?
Beth	Yes, of course. We put on a play or musical every summer, although we didn't do one last year.
Frank	Why not? What happened?
Beth	Miss Laws, the drama teacher, was out sick that semester.
Frank	What are you doing this year?
Beth	We're doing *Romeo and Juliet.*
Frank	Tell me about it.
Beth	It's a sad love story.
Frank	What are you planning for next year?
Beth	Next summer we're going to do a musical, but I don't know which one.
Frank	OK. That's great. Thanks for your help, Beth.

★★ **3** Read the conversation again. Answer the questions.

1 Why does Frank want to know about
  the drama club?
  He's writing about school clubs for the school newsletter.
2 Why wasn't there a school play last year?
  ....
3 What is the drama club going to do next year?
  ....

Speaking and Listening page 121

Brain Trainer

Guess the meaning of a new word from the context.
Read the dialogue in Exercise 4 and find the
word *detention*. What do you think it means?

a a free lesson
b extra time at school for being late, not doing
  homework, shouting in class and the like
c a box of chocolates

Look it up in a dictionary. Then do Exercise 4.

★★ **4** Complete the conversation with these phrases.
36 Then listen and check.

> ~~Tell me about it.~~
> What are you planning for the weekend?
> What did you do?
> What happened?

Dan	I'm having a bad week.
Stacey	Oh. ¹ *Tell me about it.*
Dan	On Thursday I had detention.
Stacey	Why? ² ....
Dan	I was late to school.
Stacey	Bad luck.
Dan	And yesterday I needed to go to the hospital.
Stacey	Really? ³ ....
Dan	I fell off my bike. I'm glad it's Saturday tomorrow.
Stacey	⁴ ....
Dan	I'm getting up late, and I'm staying at home. I don't want another bad day!

★★ **5** Write a conversation between you and a friend
about the week. Use the model in Exercise 4 and
the ideas below to help you.

On Thursday
  have extra homework / not pass the exam
  my best friend have a fight with me / eat all
  her candy
Yesterday
  late to school / miss the bus
  lose my bag / leave it in a café
On the Weekend
  get up early / go to the swimming pool
  go to the mall / buy a new coat

Grammar • Present continuous for future arrangements

★ 1 Choose the correct options.

1 (Are they going) / Are they go to the party on Saturday?
2 She 's staying / stays at home tomorrow.
3 They 's visiting / 're visiting their grandparents next month.
4 What does he wear / is he wearing tonight?
5 I 'm not coming / don't coming to school next week.
6 Is the train leaving / Are the train leave at 10:05?

★ 2 Complete the sentences with the correct form of the Present continuous.

1 Jon 's meeting (meet) Helen at 4 p.m.
2 The school .... (not close) early on Friday.
3 I .... (go) to the movies tonight.
4 They .... (fly) to New York next week.
5 **A** .... you .... (wear) your new pants tomorrow?
   B No, I ....
6 We .... (not play) in the tournament next weekend.
7 I .... (not go shopping) on Saturday.
8 **A** .... she .... (have) a birthday party this summer?
   B Yes, she ....

★★ 3 Look at Tammy's planner for next week. Write the questions.

Monday	write to
Tuesday	meet Sam at
Wednesday	watch the
Thursday	go to the
Friday	play basketball at
Saturday	buy a present for

1 Who is Tammy writing to on Monday?
2 When .... ?
3 What .... ?
4 Where .... ?
5 What time .... ?
6 Who .... ?

★★ 4 Look at the missing part of Tammy's planner. Answer the questions in Exercise 3.

Dev
4:30
school play
doctor's office
5:15
Luke

1 She's writing to Dev.
2 ....
3 ....
4 ....
5 ....
6 ....

★★ 5 Look at the pictures. Write sentences about Nick's vacation next week. Use these words and phrases.

fly / LA, California	go concert / park
horseback ride / mountains	surf / beach
visit wax museum / Hollywood	

Nick

Day 1 Nick's flying to LA, California.
Day 2 ....
Day 3 ....
Day 4 ....
Day 5 ....

Grammar Reference pages 102–103

Reading

1 Quickly read the page from a school textbook. Choose the best title.

1 The History of Technology
2 The Invention of Television
3 The History of Telephones

Today, people spend about seven hours every day using technology such as television, radios, MP3 players, phones and computers. Teenagers spend a lot of this time using their cell phones. Alexander Graham Bell invented the first telephone in the UK in 1876, but it was only in 1973 that Dr. Martin Cooper at Motorola invented the cell phone in the US. The phones were very big and heavy, and they were unpopular because there weren't any networks. Japan created the first network in 1979. The first cell phones only made phone calls—they didn't do anything else. Then, in 1993, people started sending text messages in Finland, and cell phones became more popular. Today, 85 percent of American adults have a cell phone, and half of British teenagers have smart phones.

Smart phones are cell phones, but you can do a lot more than make phone calls with them. You can send texts, take photos and videos, listen to the radio and connect to the Internet. When you are online, you can watch movies, send emails, play games ... and much more. In the future, smart phones are going to get thinner, like paper, and they are going to get even smarter!

2 Read the page again. Complete the information.

	Country	Year
Alexander Graham Bell invented the first telephone.	¹ *UK*	*1876*
Dr. Martin Cooper invented the cell phone.	²	
The first cellular network started.	³	
People sent text messages.	⁴	

3 Answer the questions.

1 How long do people spend using technology every day?
They spend about seven hours using technology.

2 Why didn't many people have cell phones in 1973?
....

3 How many Americans have cell phones now?
....

4 How many British teenagers have smart phones?
....

5 What can you do with a smart phone connected to the Internet?
....

6 How are smart phones going to change?
....

Listening

1 Listen to a quiz about technology. Choose
37 the correct options.

1 Who invented (television) / the telephone?
2 What's an *IM / IWB*?
3 What technology can you use to read *novels / emails*?
4 What does *LOL / WWW* stand for?
5 What are *Twitter and Facebook / broadband and Wi-Fi*?
6 Where does *Bill Gates / solar power* come from?

2 Write the answers to the questions in Exercise 1.
37 Then listen again and check.

1 *John Logie Baird.*
2 ....
3 ....
4 ....
5 ....
6 ....

Writing • A story

1 Complete the Writing File Review with these words.

> because   commas   group
> paragraphs   ~~punctuation~~

Writing File Review
Remember to use all your writing skills!

a Check your ¹ *punctuation*
Do you have periods, capital letters,
² .... , question marks
and exclamation points?

b Use linking words
Use *and*, *but* or ³ ....
to join phrases or words in a sentence.

c Write in ⁴ ....
Is the information in a ⁵ .... ?

2 Read the story. Circle the punctuation and <u>underline</u> the linking words.

Last week I dropped my cell phone on the way to school. I looked everywhere for it, but I didn't find it. My mom was very angry with me when I got home.

Yesterday a strange thing happened. My friends got a text from LeBron James. He's my favorite basketball player, and he found my phone!

I'm so happy today. I have my phone back, and LeBron sent me two tickets for the next Cleveland Cavaliers game! I'm going, with my dad, to watch them play Miami Heat next month. Can you believe it?

Darren

3 Read the story again. Are the statements true (T) or false (F)?

1 There are four paragraphs.   *F*
2 Paragraph 1 describes what happened
at the beginning of the story.   ....
3 Paragraph 2 describes what happened
last month.   ....
4 Paragraph 3 describes the end of the story.   ....
5 The story has a happy ending.   ....

4 Read the story again. Correct the sentences.

1 Darren lost his phone yesterday.
Darren lost his phone last week.
2 His mom was angry because he got home late.
....
....
3 LeBron James sent a photo to Darren's friends.
....
....
4 Darren sent LeBron two tickets.
....
....
5 Cleveland Cavaliers are going to play Miami Heat today.
....
....

5 You are going to write a story. Take notes and plan your story. Use these ideas to help you.

The object
netbook / smart phone / flash drive / e-reader

The finder
famous person / someone in your family / an alien / an animal

Think of a title for your story.

• **Paragraph 1**
What did you lose?
Where and when did you lose it?

• **Paragraph 2**
Who found it?
How did he/she contact you?

• **Paragraph 3**
What did the person who found your object do?
What is going to happen?

6 Now write your story. Use the model in Exercise 2 and your notes from Exercise 5.

....
....
....
....
....
....
....
....

Check 3

Grammar

1 **Complete the text with the Past simple of the verbs.**

Yesterday ⁰ *was* (be) great! I ¹ .... (go)
to New York for the first time. We ² ....
(take) the 9:10 train and ³ .... (arrive)
two hours later. First, we ⁴ .... (visit)
the Empire State Building. We ⁵ ....
(not eat) at the café there. We ⁶ ....
(have) some sandwiches in a park. Then we
⁷ .... (see) the musical *Aladdin*—it
⁸ .... (be) fantastic! We ⁹ ....
(get) home late. I ¹⁰ .... (not go) to bed
until 1 a.m!

/ 5 points

2 **Look at the picture. Write questions and answers.**

0 Rachel and her family / go / to New York
Did Rachel and her family go to New York?
Yes, they did.
1 they / have lunch / outside

....

2 they / wear / coats

....

3 Rachel's mom / take / any photos

....

4 there / be / any cars in the park

....

....

5 there / be / many people in the park

....

....

/ 5 points

3 **Write what the people are going to do.**

0 talk / teacher ✘   talk / her friend ✔
She isn't going to talk to the teacher.
She's going to talk to her friend.
1 buy / digital radio ✔   buy / netbook ✘
They ....
They ....
2 travel / train ✘   travel / bus ✔
I ....
I ....
3 wear / sneakers ✔   wear sandals ✘
We ....
We ....
4 download / music ✘   download / a movie ✔
He ....
He ....

/ 8 points

4 **Look at Rob's planner. What is he doing next week?**

Rob's planner

Monday	see Mr. Woods about math homework
Tuesday	visit grandpa after school
Wednesday	go to the doctor
Thursday	have extra English class at lunchtime
Friday	evening—watch World Cup at George's house
Saturday	play soccer game against Charlston

0 *On Monday he's seeing Mr. Woods about*
his math homework.
1 ....
2 ....
3 ....
4 ....
5 ....

/ 5 points

Vocabulary

5 **Complete the text with the correct transportation. Then write the date next to each picture.**

When I was five, in 1992, I got my first ⁰ b*ike*. In 2002 I got my first vehicle. It was a motor ¹ s_ _ _ _ _ _. I went to school on it. Two years later, my dad gave me my first ² c_ _. When I started my job in 2007, I bought a white ³ v_ _. I learned to drive a ⁴ t_ _ _ _ four years later. Next year I'm going to buy a ⁵ b_ _ so I can take all my friends on a trip.

0 *1992*

1 ....

2 ....

3 ....

4 ....

5 ....

/ 5 points

6 **Circle the word that doesn't fit. Then match the uncircled words to the categories (a–e).**

0 chat   charge   download   (study)   0
1 subway   blog   train   boat
2 sneakers   e-book   smart phone   Wi-Fi
3 third   sail   first   fourth
4 helicopter   ask   travel   close
5 scarf   hat   second   coat

0 technology verbs
a clothes
b verbs
c transportation
d ordinal numbers
e technology

/ 5 points

Speaking

7 **Choose the <u>incorrect</u> sentences.**

0 a I went shopping two days ago.
   b I went shopping last week.
   ⓒ I went shopping for two years.
1 a We moved here in the 1990s.
   b We moved here more than twenty years ago.
   c We moved here next month.
2 a The dog was in the backyard ten minutes ago.
   b The dog was in the backyard tomorrow.
   c The dog was in the backyard this morning.
3 a I wasn't very well last week.
   b I wasn't very well yesterday.
   c I wasn't very well soon.
4 a We stayed there for a week ago.
   b We stayed there for the weekend.
   c We stayed there for two weeks.

/ 4 points

Translation

8 **Translate the sentences.**

1 My dad's going to buy a smart phone next week.
....
2 We didn't fly in a plane; we went by helicopter.
....
3 I'm going to charge my phone tonight.
....
4 There weren't any netbooks in the 1980s.
....
5 The girl wore a blue dress and brown sandals.
....
6 I did all my homework this week.
....
7 He wore black pants and white sneakers.
....
8 My dad takes the subway to work.
....

/ 8 points

Dictation

9 **Listen and write.**
38

/ 5 points

Grammar Reference

• Have

Affirmative		
I/You/We/They	have	ice skates.
He/She/It	has	a magazine.
Negative		
I/You/We/They	don't have (do not have)	an MP3 player. a skateboard.
He/She/It	doesn't have (does not have)	
Questions and short answers		
Do I/you/we/they have a laptop?	Yes, I/you/we/they do. No, I/you/we/they don't.	
Does he/she/it have a cell phone?	Yes, he/she/it does. No, he/she/it doesn't.	

Use

• We use *have* to talk about possession.
  You have a lot of books.
  He has a blue backpack.

Form

• To form the affirmative, we use subject + *have/has*.
  *They **have** a camera.*
  *She **has** a poster of The Killers in her bedroom.*

• To form the negative, we add *don't* or *doesn't* before *have*.
  *I **don't have** a watch. (don't = do not)*
  *The car **doesn't have** a radio. (doesn't = does not)*

• The word order changes in questions:
  Do/Does + subject + have.
  ***Do** you **have** the comics?*
  ***Does** he **have** a laptop?*

• In short answers, we do not repeat *have*.
  A *Do they have a game console?*
  B *Yes, they do.*
  A *Does she have a guitar?*
  B *No, she doesn't.*

Common mistakes

He has an MP3 player. ✓
He have an MP3 player. ✗
They don't have any posters. ✓
They not have any posters. ✗

• Possessive adjectives and Possessive 's

Possessive adjectives		Possessive 's
I	my	**One person**
you	your	Paula's cat.
he	his	John's wallet.
she	her	**Two or more people**
it	its	My parents' house.
we	our	Dave and Jack's room.
they	their	

Use

We use possessive adjectives and the possessive 's to say who things belong to.

*It's **my** backpack.*
***Sam's** skateboard is green.*

Form

• We use possessive adjectives before a noun: possessive adjective + noun.
  *It's **their** dog.*

• We use **'s** after a singular noun.
  *Penny**'s** watch   my mom**'s** car*

• We use **'** after a plural noun ending in **-s**.
  *My cousins**'** house*

• We use **'s** after a plural noun not ending in **-s**.
  *the children**'s** backpacks*

Common mistake

It's Dave and Jack's room. ✓
It's Dave's and Jack's room. ✗

Grammar practice • Have

1 Rewrite the sentences. Use full forms.

1 I don't have a poster of Katy Perry.
I do not have a poster of Katy Perry.
2 She doesn't have a camera.

....
3 We don't have a big house.

....
4 He doesn't have a collection of *Star Wars* posters.

....
5 They don't have a lot of magazines.

....
6 The classroom doesn't have white walls.

....

2 Complete the sentences with *have* or *has*.

1 I *have* a big family.
2 She .... two sisters and a brother.
3 My cousin .... a black and white cat.
4 You .... a really cool hat!
5 Tracey .... long brown hair.
6 The dog .... brown eyes.

3 Look and write sentences. Use the correct form of *have*.

1 Eve / cell phone / MP3 player
Eve has a cell phone. She doesn't have an MP3 player.
2 Maria and Julia / magazine / book

....
3 Martin / soccer ball / skateboard

....
4 Ben and Leo / drinks / food

....

• Possessive adjectives

4 Write questions using *have* and the correct possessive adjective. Then write the answers.

1 he / guitar ✘
Does he have his guitar? No, he doesn't.
2 you / new CD ✔

....

....
3 the fans / cameras ✘

....

....
4 the girl / autograph book ✔

....

....
5 we / tickets for the concert ✔

....

....

• Possessive 's

5 Choose the correct options.

1 It's their *parent's /* parents' car.
2 They're my *cousin's / cousins'* cats.
3 They're *John's / Johns'* pencils.
4 It's *Mr. Black's / Mr. Blacks'* newspaper.
5 It's our *dog's / dogs'* ball.

Grammar Reference

• There is/There are; Some/Any

Singular	Plural
Affirmative	
There's (There is) a child in the park.	There are some children in the park.
Negative	
There isn't (There is not) a café in the town square.	There aren't (There are not) any cafés in the town square.
Questions and short answers	
Is there a poster on the wall?	Yes, there is. No, there isn't (there is not).
Are there any posters on the wall?	Yes, there are. No, there aren't (there are not).

Use

- We use *There is/There are* to say something exists, and *There isn't/There aren't* to say something does not exist.

- We use *There's* and *There isn't* with singular nouns.
  There's a museum next to the bank.
  There isn't a library.

- We use *There are* and *There aren't* with plural nouns.
  There are twenty stores in the mall.
  There aren't any trains today.

- We use *some* in affirmative sentences.
  There are **some** tickets for the concert.

- We use *any* in negative sentences and questions.
  There aren't **any** books in my backpack.
  Are there **any** strawberries in the fridge?

Form

- To form the affirmative, we use *There + is/are*.
  There's a swimming pool in the sports complex.
  There are some beautiful parks in the city.

- To form the negative, we add *not* after *There is/are*.
  There isn't a café at the station. (= There is not)
  There aren't any French students in our class.
  (= There are not)

- The word order changes in questions: *Is/Are + there*.
  Is there a hospital near here?
  Are there any keys on the table?

Common mistakes
There's a cat in the tree. ✓
~~Is a cat in the tree.~~ ✗
There isn't a laptop on the desk. ✓
~~There no is a laptop on the desk.~~ ✗

• *Can/Can't* for ability

Affirmative		
I/You/He/She/It/We/They	can	juggle.
Negative		
I/You/He/She/It/We/They	can't (cannot)	dance.
Questions and short answers		
Can I/you/he/she/it/we/they skate?	Yes, I/you/he/she/it/we/they can. No, I/you/he/she/it/we/they can't (cannot).	

Use

- We use *can* to talk about ability.
  I **can** play the guitar.
  He **can't** ride a bike.

Form

- To form the affirmative, we use *can* + main verb.
  We **can swim**.

- To form the negative, we add *not* after *can*.
  The short form of *cannot* is *can't*.
  She **can't dance**.

- The word order changes in questions:
  Can + subject + main verb.
  Can you sing?

- In short answers, we do not repeat the main verb.
  A Can it fly? **B** Yes, it can.

Common mistake
He can skate. ✓
~~He can to skate.~~ ✗

Grammar practice • There is/ There are; Some/Any

1 Match the stores (A–D) to the descriptions (1–3). Complete the descriptions with *There is/isn't* or *There are/aren't.*

1 ☐ In this store, you can buy furniture.
   ¹ *There are* some tables and chairs.
   ² .... a big desk, but
   ³ .... any beds.
2 ☐ In this store, ⁴ .... a lot of DVDs. ⁵ .... a lot of CDs too, but ⁶ .... any DVD or CD players.
3 ☐ In this store, ⁷ .... a lot of toys. ⁸ .... a tepee and a kite, but ⁹ .... a bike.

2 Complete the description of the fourth picture.

| books | computer | interactive whiteboard |
| magazines | ~~pens~~ | |

In this store, there are a lot of ¹ *pens* and
² ...., but there aren't any
³ .... There's a
⁴ ...., but there isn't an
⁵ ....

3 Answer the questions about the pictures in Exercise 1.

1 Is there a computer in one of the stores?
   Yes, there is.
2 Is there a girl in the DVD store?
   ....
3 Are there any children in the toy store?
   ....
4 Are there any people in the furniture store?
   ....

4 Write sentences using *There is/are* or *There isn't/aren't.*

1 mountains / my country ✓
   There are some mountains in my country.
2 museum / my town ✗
   ....
3 library / my school ✓
   ....
4 pets / my house ✗
   ....

• Can/Can't for ability

5 Match the sentences (1–4) to the people.

	⛸	🏊	🤹	🚲	🎾
Andrew	✗	✓	✗	✓	✗
Ben	✓	✓	✗	✓	✓
Charlie	✗	✗	✗	✓	✓
Dave	✗	✓	✓	✓	✓

1 He can't skate, but he can juggle and bike.
   Dave
2 He can skate and play tennis, but he can't juggle.
3 He can swim and bike, but he can't play tennis.
4 He can bike and play tennis, but he can't swim.

6 Answer the questions about the people in Exercise 5.

1 Who can juggle?   *Dave*
2 Who can't play tennis?   ....
3 Who can't swim?   ....
4 Who can skate?   ....
5 What can they all do?   ....

7 Answer the questions with full sentences.

1 Who can drive in your family?
   My mom and dad can drive.
2 What water sports can you do?
   ....
3 What languages can you speak?
   ....
4 What musical instrument can you play?
   ....

Grammar Reference

• Present simple: affirmative and negative

Affirmative		
I/You/We/They	start	school at 9 a.m.
He/She/It	gets up	early.
Negative		
I/You/We/They	don't (do not)	take a shower in the morning.
He/She/It	doesn't (does not)	go to bed early.

Time expressions

every day
every Monday
on the weekend
after school
on Mondays
at nine o'clock

Use

We use the Present simple to talk about:

• routines and habits.
  *He **gets up** at 7 a.m. every day.*

• things that are true in general.
  *We **live** in a small town.*

Form

• To form the third person singular (with *he*, *she* and *it*), we add **-s**, **-es** or **-ies** to the verb. (See **Spelling rules**.)
  *She speak**s** Spanish.*

• To form the negative, we use *do not (don't) with I, you, we* and *they*. We use *does not (doesn't) with he, she* and *it*.
  *We **don't** have dinner together.*
  *He **doesn't** do Sudoku puzzles.*

• We use time expressions to say when or how often we do something.
  *She plays soccer **on Saturdays**.*

• The time expression usually goes at the end of the sentence.
  *Eric goes to bed **at 9:30 p.m.***

• Spelling rules: verb + -s

most verbs: add **-s**	read → reads play → plays
verbs that end in **-ss**, **-ch**, **-sh**, **-x** and **-o**: add **-es**	kiss → kisses watch → watches wash → washes fix → fixes go → goes
verbs that end in a consonant + **y**: drop the **y** and add **-ies**	study → studies

Common mistakes

He goes to bed early. ✓
~~He go to bed early.~~ ✗
She doesn't eat pizza. ✓
~~She doesn't eats pizza.~~ ✗

• Present simple: questions and short answers

Questions and short answers	
Do I/you/we/they live downtown?	Yes, I/you/we/they do. No, I/you/we/they don't.
Does he/she/it like music?	Yes, he/she/it does. No, he/she/it doesn't.

Negative		
I/You/We/They	don't (do not)	take a shower in the morning.
He/She/It	doesn't (does not)	go to bed early.

Form

• To form questions, we use *do* with *I, you, we* and *they*. We use *does* with *he, she* and *it*. The word order also changes: *Do/Does* + subject + main verb.
  ***Do** they **walk** to school?*
  ***Does** she **speak** English?*

• In short answers, we do not repeat the main verb.
  A ***Does** he **brush** his teeth in the morning?*
  B *Yes, he **does**.*

Common mistake

A *Does he play the guitar?*   **B** *Yes, he does.* ✓
A *Does he play the guitar?*   **B** *~~Yes, he plays.~~* ✗

Grammar practice • Present simple: affirmative and negative

1 Complete the sentences. Use the Present simple of the verbs and these words.

| her homework | my friends | ~~our teeth~~ |
| tennis | TV | |

1 We *brush our teeth* (brush) after breakfast.
2 They .... (play) every day.
3 She .... (do) at home.
4 He .... (watch) in the evening.
5 I .... (meet) in the park.

2 Complete the text. Use the Present simple of the verbs.

I ¹ *like* (like) geography a lot because we ² .... (learn) about other countries. Our project this year is about South America. People ³ .... (speak) Spanish in many South American countries. My mom ⁴ .... (come) from South America, but she ⁵ .... (not speak) Spanish because she's Brazilian. The people in Brazil ⁶ .... (not speak) Spanish. They ⁷ .... (speak) Portuguese.

3 Look at the pictures. Correct the sentences.

1 Barry gets up at eight o'clock.
Barry doesn't get up at eight o'clock.
He gets up at seven o'clock.
2 He has breakfast with his dad.
....
3 He bikes to school.
....
4 Classes start at ten o'clock.
....

4 Rewrite the sentences for you. Make them true.

Isabelle

1 Isabelle goes to school by bus.
I go to school by car.
I don't go to school by bus.
2 She likes math.
....
....
3 She watches TV in bed.
....
....
4 She doesn't get up early on the weekend.
....
....

• Present simple: questions and short answers

5 Put the words in the correct order to make questions.

1 at / open / half past nine? / Does / library / the
Does the library open at half past nine?
2 their / Mimi and Noah / friends / meet / school? / Do / after
.... ?
3 Thursdays? / Do / science / have / they / on
.... ?
4 his / clean up / Does / room / he / the / weekend? / on
.... ?
5 go / Does / to / before / sister / bed / your / you?
.... ?

6 Write questions. Then answer the questions for you.

1 you (bike) to school in the morning
Do you bike to school in the morning?
Yes, I do./No, I don't.
2 students (study) computer science at your school
.... ?
....
3 your school day (start) at 8 a.m.
.... ?
....
4 you (wear) a uniform
.... ?
....

Grammar Reference

• Adverbs of frequency

0%		50%			100%
never	hardly ever	sometimes	often	usually	always

I always get up at 6:30.
I hardly ever watch TV.
I am sometimes very tired.

Use

- We often use adverbs of frequency with the Present simple to say how often we do something.
  I **always** do my homework.

- Adverbs of frequency usually go:
  – before the main verb.
  Goats **sometimes** climb trees.

  – after the verb *to be*.
  My dog is **never** sad.

Common mistakes

I never play soccer. ✓
~~I play never soccer.~~ ✗
She's always tired. ✓
~~Always she is tired.~~ ✗

• Present simple with *Wh* questions

Wh questions
Where do you live?   In Mexico.
When does the movie end?   At nine o'clock.
What does she eat for lunch?   Sandwiches.
Who do you meet on the way to school?   Lauren and Wendy.
Why does he get up late?   Because he works at night.
How often do they go to the movies?   Every week!

Use

- We use *where* to ask about place.
  Where is the train station?

- We use *when* to ask about time.
  When does the party start?

- We use *what* to ask about things.
  What do you have in your bag?

- We use *who* to ask about people.
  Who can juggle six balls?

- We use *why* to ask the reason for something.
  Why are you late?

- We use *how often* to ask how frequently something happens.
  How often do you clean up your room?

Form

- To form questions with most verbs, we use this word order: *Wh* question word + *do/does* + subject + main verb.
  What does she like?

- To form questions with *to be* and modal verbs, we use inversion.
  Where are you?
  What can she do?

Common mistakes

When do you go to bed? ✓
~~When you go to bed?~~ ✗
~~When go you to bed?~~ ✗

• Must/Mustn't

Affirmative		
I/You/He/She/It/We/They	must	listen to her.
Negative		
I/You/He/She/It/We/They	mustn't (must not)	use cell phones in class.

Use

- We use *must* to talk about important rules.
  I **must** do my homework.

- We use *mustn't* to talk about things we are not allowed to do.
  You **mustn't** eat in class.

Form

- To form the affirmative, we use subject + *must* + main verb.
  They **must** keep the dog on a leash.

- To form the negative, we add *not* after *must*.
  They **mustn't** use cell phones in class. (= must not)

Common mistakes

You mustn't play soccer in the park. ✓
~~You mustn't to play soccer in the park.~~ ✗
~~You mustn't talking in the library.~~ ✗

Grammar practice • Adverbs of frequency

1. Look at the information in the table. Write the correct name next to each sentence.

Will	20%	50%	50%	60%	100%
Zoe	0%	20%	60%	20%	100%
Luke	100%	0%	60%	0%	80%

1 I never feed the fish.   *Zoe*
2 I sometimes go horseback
   riding.   ....
3 I hardly ever clean out the rabbits'
   hutch.   ....
4 I usually take the dog for a walk.   ....
5 I often play with the cat.   ....
6 I always give the fish some food.   ....

2. Look at the information in Exercise 1. Answer the questions with full sentences.

1 How often does Will feed the fish?
   He hardly ever feeds the fish.
2 How often do Luke and Zoe go horseback riding?
   ....
3 How often does Luke play with the cat?
   ....
4 How often does Will clean out the rabbits' hutch?
   ....
5 How often do Zoe and Will take the dog for a walk?
   ....

• Present simple with *Wh* questions

3. Circle the question words. Then translate them.

1 Who   ....
2 Where   ....
3 Have   ....
4 Will   ....
5 When   ....
6 White   ....
7 What   ....
8 How   ....
9 Has   ....
10 Why   ....

4. Match the question words (1–6) to the question endings (a–f). Then choose the correct options.

1 Who *f*   a *is / does* the movie start?
2 When   b *is / does* the sports complex?
3 How often   c *are / do* your favorite subjects?
4 Why   d *are / do* you go shopping?
5 What   e *isn't / doesn't* your dog here?
6 Where   f *(is) / do* your favorite actor?

• Must/Mustn't

5. Complete the sentences.

clean up my room	close the gates
eat in class	hurt the animals
jump on my bed	listen to the teacher

1 At home, I must ....
   I mustn't ....
2 At school, we must ....
   We mustn't ....
3 On a farm, you must ....
   You mustn't ....

6. Look at the pictures. Write sentences using *must/mustn't*.

wear / warm clothes	stand under / tree
~~swim / ocean~~	walk / mountains

In bad weather:

1 *You mustn't swim
  in the ocean.*

2 ....
  ....

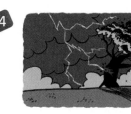

3 ....
  ....

4 ....
  ....

Grammar Reference

• Present continuous

Affirmative		
I	'm (am)	reading.
He/She/It	is	reading.
You/We/They	're (are)	reading.
Negative		
I	'm not (am not)	playing.
He/She/It	isn't (is not)	playing.
You/We/They	aren't (are not)	playing.
Questions and short answers		
Am I singing?	Yes, I am. / No, I'm not.	
Is he/she/it singing?	Yes, he/she/it is. No, he/she/it isn't.	
Are you/we/they singing?	Yes, you/we/they are. No, you/we/they aren't.	
***Wh* questions**		
What are you watching?		

Time expressions
(right) now
today
at the moment

Use

• We use the Present continuous to talk about actions that are happening now.
She's playing the guitar at the moment.

Form

• We form the Present continuous with *to be* (*am, is* or *are*) + main verb + **-ing**.
They're making a cake.

• To form the negative, we add *not* after *am, is* or *are*.
The dog isn't swimming in the ocean. (= is not)

• The word order changes in questions: *Am/Is/Are* + subject + main verb + **-ing**.
Are you painting a picture of your sister?

• In short answers, we do not repeat the main verb.
A *Is he climbing that mountain?*   **B** *Yes, he is.*

• Spelling rules: verb + *-ing*

most verbs: add **-ing**	play → playing
verbs that end in **-e**: drop the **-e** and add **-ing**	come → coming
verbs that end in one vowel + one consonant: double the consonant and add **-ing**	sit → sitting

Common mistakes
He's dancing. ✓
He dancing. ✗
Are they talking? ✓
They are talking? ✗
We're watching a movie. ✓
We're watch a movie. ✗

• Present simple and Present continuous

Present simple	Present continuous
I often swim here.	I'm looking at the animals now.

Use
Present simple
We use the Present simple to talk about:

• routines and habits.
I go to the movies every weekend.

• things that are true in general.
Goats live in the mountains.

• Time expressions:
adverbs of frequency *(never, hardly ever, sometimes, usually/often, always), every day/week/month, every Saturday, on the weekend, after school, on Wednesday at two o'clock*

Present continuous

• We use the Present continuous to talk about things that are happening now.
She's watching her favorite TV show at the moment.

• Time expressions: *now, today, at the moment*

Common mistake
I usually do gymnastics on Mondays, but today I'm playing basketball. ✓

I usually am doing gymnastics but today I play basketball. ✗

Grammar practice • Present continuous

1 Complete the table with the -ing form of these verbs.

drink	get	go	have	jump	make
run	sit	swim	take	watch	write

+ -ing	e + -ing	x2 + -ing
drinking	*having*	*getting*
....	....	....
....	....	....
....	....	....

2 Look at the picture. Complete the sentences with these verbs. Then write the names on the picture.

drive	eat	snow	take	talk	wear

1 It's *snowing* in the mountains.
2 Becky .... a photo.
3 Oliver .... his car.
4 Becky and I .... warm clothes.
5 Bill and Amanda .... lunch.
6 I .... on my cell phone.

3 Complete the conversation with the Present continuous of the verbs.

Dad What ¹ *are you reading* (you / read)?
Fred I ² .... (not read).
I ³ .... (look) for a word in this dictionary.
Dad What subject ⁴ .... (you / study)?
Fred I ⁵ .... (study) English right now. We ⁶ .... (learn) the words for different outdoor activities, and I ⁷ .... (write) about my favorite activities.

4 Complete the questions. Then match the questions (1–5) to the answers (a–e).

1 What *are you doing* (you / do)?   d
2 Where .... (you / go)?
3 Who .... (you / sit) next to?
4 Why .... (they / open) the window?
5 When .... (we / arrive)?

a To New Haven.
b At 4:15.
c Because it's hot.
d I'm sitting on a train.
e My sister.

• Present simple and Present continuous

5 Rewrite the sentences using the correct time expression.

1 We're playing baseball. (every week / now)
We're playing baseball now.
2 The children go kayaking. (usually / at the moment)
....
3 She isn't swimming in the ocean. (never / at the moment)
....
4 I'm taking the dog for a walk. (today / every day)
....
5 You don't sing in the shower. (tonight / often)
....

6 Complete the sentences and questions. Use the Present simple or Present continuous.

1 I'm *not watching* (not watch) TV at the moment.
2 Dr. Barrett .... (go) to the hospital every morning.
3 .... (it / rain) now?
4 They .... (not get up) early on the weekend.
5 .... (she / swim) in the ocean in the summer?
6 Who .... (we / wait) for?

Grammar Reference

• Countable and uncountable nouns

Countable nouns		Uncountable nouns
Singular	**Plural**	some bread
a sandwich	some sandwiches	some pasta
a tomato	some tomatoes	some rice
an apple	some apples	some water

Form

- Countable nouns can be singular or plural.
  egg → eggs   vegetable → vegetables
- Uncountable nouns have no plural form.
  juice, pasta, water
- We use *a* before singular countable nouns starting with a consonant sound.
  a potato, a sandwich
- We use *an* before singular countable nouns starting with a vowel sound.
  an apple, an orange
- We can use *some* before plural countable nouns and uncountable nouns.
  some tomatoes, some chicken

• Many/Much/A lot of

How many?	How much?
How many bananas do you have?	How much yogurt do you have?
We don't have any bananas.	We don't have any yogurt.
We don't have many bananas.	We don't have much yogurt.
We have some/four bananas.	We have some yogurt.
We have a lot of bananas.	We have a lot of yogurt.

Use

- We can use *many*, *some* and *a lot of* with countable nouns.
  *many apples, **some** apples, **a lot of** apples*
- We can use *much*, *some* and *a lot of* with uncountable nouns.
  *much pasta, **some** pasta, **a lot of** pasta*
- We use *How much?* and *How many?* to ask about quantities.
  How much water is there?
  How many friends do you have?

- We usually use *a lot of* in affirmative sentences.
  *There are **a lot of** books on the table.*
- We usually use *much* and *many* in negative sentences and questions.
  *There isn't **much** juice.*
  *Do you have **many** pets?*

• Comparatives

Short adjectives	Comparatives
old	older (than)
hot	hotter (than)
nice	nicer (than)
happy	happier (than)
Long adjectives	**Comparatives**
popular	more popular (than)
interesting	more interesting (than)
Irregular adjectives	**Comparatives**
good	better (than)
bad	worse (than)

Use

- We use comparative adjectives to compare two people or things.
  *The café is **cheaper** than the restaurant.*

Form

Short adjectives	Comparatives
most adjectives: add **-er**	small → smaller
adjectives that end in **-e**: add **-r**	nice → nicer
adjectives that end in one vowel + one consonant: double the consonant and add **-er**	hot → hotter
adjectives that end in **-y**: drop the **y** and add **-ier**	pretty → prettier
Long adjectives	
add **more**	interesting → more interesting
irregular adjectives	good → better bad → worse

Grammar practice • Countable and uncountable nouns

1 Write Countable (C) or Uncountable (U).

1 time	*U*	6 watches	*C*
2 butter	....	7 eggs	....
3 lake	....	8 water	....
4 wallet	....	9 money	....
5 music	....	10 songs	....

• Many/Much/A lot of

2 Complete the questions with *How much* or *How many*.

1 *How much* bread do we have?
2 .... bananas are there?
3 .... rice is there?
4 .... apples do we have?
5 .... eggs do we need?
6 .... milk is in the fridge?

3 Look at the picture and the table. Write sentences.

There	's isn't are aren't	a lot of much many	cheese sandwiches fruit sausage juice chips

1 *There isn't much cheese.*
2 ....
3 ....
4 ....
5 ....
6 ....

• Comparatives

4 Choose the correct options. Then match the sentences (1–5) to the rules (a–e) and write the base adjective.

1 Debbie's (thinner)/ thiner than Rodney.   c
2 Laura's *happyer* / *happier* than Katie.
3 Peter's *interestingger* / *more interesting* than James.
4 Paul's *taller* / *tallr* than Yvonne.
5 Jane's *nicer* / *more nice* than her sister.

a *more* + long adjective   ....
b + *-er*   ....
c x2 + *-er*   *thin*
d + *-r*   ....
e *-y* + *-ier*   ....

5 Look at the pictures. Complete the sentences.

1 **old**
  The man in B *is older than the man in A.*
2 **hot**
  The cup of coffee in B ....
3 **thin**
  The woman in B ....
4 **large**
  The salad in B ....
5 **dirty**
  The boy in B ....

Grammar Reference

Past simple: *to be*

Affirmative		
I/He/She/It	was	in the library.
You/We/They	were	in the library.
Negative		
I/He/She/It	wasn't (was not)	in the backyard.
You/We/They	weren't (were not)	in the backyard.
Questions and short answers	
Was I/he/she/it noisy?	Yes, I/he/she/it was. / No, I/he/she/it wasn't (was not).
Were you/we/they dirty?	Yes, you/we/they were. / No, you/we/they weren't (were not).

Time expressions

yesterday   a week ago   yesterday morning
in 1845   last month

Use

- We use the Past simple to talk about states (or actions) that began and finished in the past.
  *They **were** at home yesterday.*

Form

- To form the affirmative, we use subject + *was/were*.
  *I **was** at the library.   We **were** on the train.*

- To form the negative, we add *not* after *was/were*.
  *It **wasn't** very expensive. (= was not)*

- The word order changes in questions: *Was/Were* + subject.
  Was he happy?   Were they late?

There was/There were

Affirmative
There was a movie/some juice.
There were some comics.
Negative
There wasn't a museum/any coffee.
There weren't any magazines.
Questions and short answers	
Was there a bus station/any tea?	Yes, there was.
Were there any books?	No, there weren't.

Use

- We use *there was/were* to say something existed or didn't exist in the past.
  *There **was** color TV twenty years ago.*
  *There **weren't** any interactive whiteboards in 1990.*

- We use *there was* and *there wasn't* with singular and uncountable nouns.
  *There **was** a movie theater in the shopping mall.*
  *There **wasn't** any pasta in the store.*

- We use *there were/weren't* with plural nouns.
  *There **were** some good shows on TV last week.*
  *There **weren't** many cars on our street fifty years ago.*

Form

- To form the affirmative, we use *there* + *was/were*.
  *There **was** a poster of the Beatles on his wall.*
  *There **were** some famous models in the 1960s.*

- To form the negative, we add *not* after *was/were*.
  *There **wasn't** a phone booth near our house.*
  *There **weren't** any cell phones in the 1960s.*

- To form questions, we use *Was/Were* + *there*.
  Was there a school trip to New Orleans last year?
  Were there any DVDs five years ago?

Past simple: regular affirmative and negative

Affirmative		
I/You/He/She/It/We/They	lived	in an old house.
Negative		
I/You/He/She/It/We/They	didn't (did not) live	in an old house.

Use

- We use the Past simple to talk about states or actions that began and finished in the past.
  *She **listened** to the radio.*

Form

- To form the Past simple of regular verbs, we add **-ed**, **-d** or **-ied** to the verb. (See Spelling rules.)
  *He **asked** questions about the 1950s.*

- To form the negative of regular verbs, we use *didn't (did not)* + the main verb in the infinitive.
  *She **didn't answer** the phone.*

- We use time expressions to say <u>when</u> we did something. The time expression goes at the beginning or at the end of the sentence.
*They traveled to Texas **last night**.*
In the 1870s, Mr. Bell invented the telephone.

Spelling rules: verb + -ed

most verbs: add **-ed**	jump → jumped visit → visited
verbs that end in **-e**: add **-d**	live → lived die → died
verbs that end in consonant + **-y**: drop the **y** and add **-ied**	carry → carried study → studied
verbs that end in one vowel + one consonant: double the consonant and add **-ed**	drop → dropped

Grammar practice • Past simple: *to be*

1 Complete the conversation with *was, wasn't, were* or *weren't*.

Anna Where ¹ *were* you yesterday?
You ² .... at home.
Rosie No, I ³ .... I ⁴ ....
at Mario's, the Italian restaurant we like,
because it ⁵ .... my dad's birthday.
Anna How ⁶ .... it?
Rosie The food ⁷ .... delicious, but
the waiter ⁸ .... great.
⁹ .... you and Daisy at Carol's?
Anna No, we ¹⁰ .... Carol
¹¹ .... at her grandpa's house,
and Daisy and I ¹² .... at home.
Friends ¹³ .... on TV last night,
so we watched that.

There was/There were

2 Look at the shopping list and the basket, and write what was in the grocery store. Use *There was/wasn't, There were/weren't*.

eggs bananas chocolate magazine water	1 *There weren't any eggs.* 2 .... 3 .... 4 .... 5 ....

3 Look at the picture of Nina's grandma fifty years ago. Complete Nina's questions using *Was there/ Were there*. Write her grandma's answers.

1 *Was there* a telephone in the house?
Yes, there was.
2 .... any DVDs?
....
3 .... any books or magazines?
....
4 .... a game console?
....

Past simple regular: affirmative and negative

4 Complete the table with the Past simple of these verbs.

carry	chop	~~close~~	~~cook~~	dance	drop
like	listen	start	~~stop~~	~~study~~	try

+ -ed	x2 + -ed	+ -d	-y + -ied
cooked	stopped	closed	studied
....	....	....	....
....	....	....	....

5 Complete the sentences with the Past simple of the verbs. Write one affirmative and one negative sentence.

1 visit
We *didn't visit* the museum yesterday.
We *visited* our grandparents in the evening.
2 study
He .... French last year
because he wants to live in France.
Jessica .... literature because
she doesn't like reading.
3 stop
The bus .... near my house,
so I got home late again.
It .... next to the park.

Grammar Reference

• Past simple irregular: affirmative and negative

Affirmative		
I/You/He/She/It/We/They	had	breakfast.
Negative		
I/You/He/She/It/We/They	didn't (did not) have	breakfast.

Time expressions

yesterday   yesterday morning   last month

a week ago   in 1845

Use

- We use the Past simple to talk about states or actions that began and finished in the past.
  *They **flew** to the US.*
  *He **didn't understand** the question.*

Form

- We don't add **-s** to the third person (***he/she/it***) in the Past simple.
  *He **did** his homework.*

- To form the negative of irregular verbs, we use *did not (didn't)* + the main verb in the infinitive.
  *We **didn't go** to school yesterday.*

- We use time expressions to say <u>when</u> we did something.
  *She bought a new car **last weekend**.*

- The time expression goes at the beginning or the end of the sentence.
  *Peter ran a marathon **two years ago**.*
  ***Two years ago**, Peter ran a marathon.*

• Past simple: questions

Regular verbs	
Did I/you/he/she/it/we/they visit the museum?	Yes, I/you/he/she/it/we/they did. No, I/you/he/she/it/we/they didn't.
Irregular verbs	
Did I/you/he/she/it/we/they see the Eiffel Tower?	Yes, I/you/he/she/it/we/they did. No, I/you/he/she/it/we/they didn't.
Wh questions	
How did you travel? What did they do?	

Form

- To form questions, we use *Did* + the main verb in the infinitive. The word order also changes:
  Did + subject + main verb.
  ***Did** they **sail** to Spain?*
  ***Did** she **lose** her ticket?*

- In short answers, we do not repeat the main verb.
  A *Did* you *enjoy* the movie?   **B** *Yes, I did.*

Common mistake

Did they like the movie? ✓
~~Did they liked the movie?~~ ✗

Grammar practice • Past simple
irregular: affirmative and negative

1 Complete the sentences with the Past simple of these verbs.

> drink   get up   go   have   ~~understand~~

1 I *understood* the question.
2 She .... at seven thirty yesterday.
3 We .... lunch at one thirty in the café in the town square.
4 They .... to the Empire State Building.
5 He .... two bottles of water because he was thirsty.

2 Rewrite the text in the Past simple.

Every year we [1] **go** to the beach in the summer, and we [2] **take** our dog, Trixie. We [3] **put** her in the back of the car. My mom [4] **drives,** and my dad [5] **reads** the map and [6] **tells** her where to go. We [7] **have** lunch on the way there. We [8] **eat** the picnic lunch that Mom [9] **makes** for the trip. It [10] **'s** a long trip, and we [11] **are** happy when we [12] **arrive** in the evening.

Last year we went to the beach ....

....

....

....

....

....

....

....

....

3 Write negative sentences using the Past simple.

1 we / not see / any sharks
We didn't see any sharks.
2 he / not eat / the ice cream
....
3 there / not be / any boats
....
4 they / not play / beach volleyball
....
5 the children / not make / sandcastles
....

4 Correct the sentences.

1 Their parents got up early. (late)
Their parents didn't get up early.
They got up late.
2 Paul saw a dolphin. (big fish)
....
3 I swam in the swimming pool. (ocean)
....
4 Martha rode a pony. (horse)
....
5 The family had fish for dinner. (pizza)
....

• Past simple: questions

5 Mark the correct questions.

1 a Did you stay in Los Angeles?   ☑
  b Did you stayed in Los Angeles?   ☐
2 a Visited they the zoo?   ☐
  b Did they visit the zoo?   ☐
3 a Did he goes to Hollywood?   ☐
  b Did he go to Hollywood?   ☐
4 a Did she ate a hamburger?   ☐
  b Did she eat a hamburger?   ☐
5 a What did we see in the aquarium?   ☐
  b What saw we in the aquarium?   ☐

6 Write questions to ask Dan about his vacation. Then look at the picture and write his answers.

Eiffel Tower

TRAIN TICKET
TRAIN TICKET
TRAIN TICKET
TRAIN TICKET
Destination: PARIS
Date: 17 August

1 where / go
Where did you go on vacation?
I went to Paris.
2 how / travel
....
....
3 when / arrive
....
....
4 who / go with
....
....

Grammar Reference

• Be going to

Affirmative		
I	'm (am) going to	start a blog tomorrow.
He/She/It	's (is) going to	start a blog tomorrow.
You/We/They	're (are) going to	start a blog tomorrow.

Negative		
I	'm not (am not) going to	buy an e-book.
He/She/It	isn't (is not) going to	buy an e-book.
You/We/They	're not (are not) going to	buy an e-book.

Questions and short answers	
Am I going to have broadband?	Yes, I am. / No, I'm not.
Is he/she/it going to have broadband?	Yes, he/she/it is. No, he/she/it isn't.
Are you/we/they going to have broadband?	Yes, you/we/they are. No, you/we/they aren't.

Wh questions
What are you going to do tomorrow?

Time expressions

tomorrow	next week	next month
next year	soon	at two o'clock

Use

- We use *be going to* to talk about plans and intentions for the future.
  She's going to take a flash drive to school.

Form

- To form the affirmative, we use the verb *to be* (**am**, **is** or **are**) + **going to** + main verb.
  I'm going to write an email this evening.

- To form the negative, we add *not* after *am, is* or *are.*
  We aren't going to watch TV. (= are not)

- The word order changes in questions:
  am/is/are + subject + **going to** + main verb.
  Is he going to buy a netbook tomorrow?

- In short answers, we do not repeat the main verb.
  A *Are you going to ask about broadband?*
  B *No, I'm not.*

• Present continuous for future arrangements

Affirmative		
I	'm (am) having	a party tonight.
He/She/It	's (is) having	a party tonight.
You/We/They	're (are) having	a party tonight.

Negative		
I	'm not (am not) flying	to the US next week.
He/She/It	isn't (is not) flying	to the US next week.
You/We/They	're not (are not) flying	to the US next week.

Questions and short answers	
Am I staying at your house tomorrow?	Yes, I am. / No, I'm not.
Is he/she/it staying at your house tomorrow?	Yes, he/she/it is. No, he/she/it isn't.
Are you/we/they staying at your house tomorrow?	Yes, you/we/they are. No, you/we/they aren't.

Wh questions
Where are you going on Tuesday?

Time expressions

at nine o'clock	tomorrow	tomorrow evening
on Thursday	this afternoon	next weekend

Use

- We use the Present continuous to talk about future arrangements.
  I'm playing in a basketball game at three.

Grammar practice • Be going to

1 Write what each person is going to do.
Use these phrases.

> charge his cell phone   play computer games
> read my e-book   send a text message
> ~~use a search engine~~

1 He *'s going to use a search engine.*
2 They ....
3 I ....
4 He ....
5 She ....

2 Complete the text with the correct form
of *be going to*.

This Saturday, Paul, Ted and Josh [1] *are going to
play* (play) with their band in the town square.
Their friend, Becky, [2] .... (sing).
The concert [3] .... (not start) until
9 p.m.
There [4] .... (not be) any food,
but there [5] .... (be) a lot of drinks
for sale. All their friends [6] .... (go).
Ted's dad [7] .... (make) a video, and
they [8] .... (put) it on the Internet.

3 Read the answers and write questions.

> bank   ~~movie theater~~   post office
> supermarket   train station

1 *Are they going to go to the movie theater?*
   Yes. They're going to see a movie.
2 .... ?
   Yes. She's going to get some money.
3 .... ?
   Yes. I'm going to send some letters.
4 .... ?
   Yes. He's going to take the train to Boston.
5 .... ?
   Yes. They're going to buy some food.

• Present continuous for future arrangements

4 Mark the sentences about the future.

1 I'm flying to Greece tomorrow. ☑
2 At the moment, they're playing baseball
   in the park. ☐
3 Are you going to the dentist next week? ☐
4 The train's leaving this afternoon at
   four thirty. ☐
5 She's wearing a red dress and brown
   sandals today. ☐
6 Is he studying in his room? ☐

5 Complete the sentences with the Present
continuous of the <u>underlined</u> verbs.

1 We <u>don't go skiing</u> in the spring. We *aren't
   going skiing* next month.
2 The planes <u>fly</u> to the US every day. The planes
   .... to the US tonight.
3 They <u>watch</u> TV in the evenings. They
   .... TV after dinner.
4 He <u>doesn't play</u> any sports. He
   .... soccer tomorrow.
5 I often <u>meet</u> my friends in the park.
   I .... them in the park
   after school.
6 She <u>stays</u> with her grandma every summer.
   She .... with her grandma
   next July.

6 Complete the questions.

1 Who *are you seeing* tomorrow?
   I'm seeing Dr. White.
2 Where .... on the weekend?
   He's going to San Francisco.
3 When .... ?
   They're coming back on Thursday.
4 What .... to the party
   on Friday?
   She's wearing her new green dress.
5 .... tonight?
   Yes. We're watching *Friends* on NBC.
6 What exams .... tomorrow?
   They're taking their Spanish and history exams.

Vocabulary

My World

Unit vocabulary

1 Translate the words.

Objects

camera ....
cell phone ....
comics ....
DVD ....
game console ....
guitar ....
ice skates ....
laptop ....
magazine ....
MP3 player ....
poster ....
skateboard ....
wallet ....
watch ....

2 Translate the words.

Adjectives

bad ....
big ....
boring ....
cheap ....
difficult ....
easy ....
expensive ....
good ....
interesting ....
new ....
old ....
popular ....
small ....
unpopular ....

Vocabulary extension

3 Match the photos to the words in the box. Use your dictionary if necessary. Write the words in English and in your language.

| alarm clock | bike helmet | ~~bracelets~~ | hairbrush | keys |

1 ....*bracelets*...........................

2 ....

3 ....

4 ....

5 ....
....

Vocabulary

Unit vocabulary

1 Translate the words.

Places in a town

bank ....

bus station ....

café ....

hospital ....

library ....

movie theater

....

museum ....

park ....

police station

....

post office ....

shopping mall

....

sports complex ....

town square ....

train station ....

2 Translate the words.

Action verbs

bike ....

climb ....

dance ....

fly ....

juggle ....

jump ....

play ....

run ....

sing ....

skate ....

swim ....

walk ....

Vocabulary extension

3 Match the photos to the words in the box. Use your dictionary if necessary. Write the words in English and in your language.

| art gallery | ~~bookstore~~ | restaurant | supermarket | theater |

1 _bookstore_ ....   2 ....

3 ....   4 ....

5 ....
....

Vocabulary

Unit vocabulary

1 Translate the phrases.

Daily routines

brush my teeth

....

clean up my room

....

do homework ....

get dressed ....

get up ....

go home ....

go to bed ....

have breakfast ....

have dinner ....

have lunch ....

meet friends ....

start school ....

take a shower ....

watch TV ....

2 Translate the words and phrases.

School subjects

art ....

computer science

....

English ....

French ....

geography ....

history ....

literature ....

math ....

music ....

PE (physical education)

....

science ....

social studies ....

Vocabulary extension

3 Match the photos to the words in the box. Use your dictionary if necessary. Write the words in English and in your language.

| bell | lunch box | pencil case | ~~schedule~~ | textbook |

1 ....*schedule*....... ....

2 ....

3 ....

4 ....

5 ....
....

Vocabulary

Animal Magic

Unit vocabulary

1 **Translate the words.**

Unusual animals

frog ....
giant rabbit ....
hissing cockroach
....
lizard ....
parrot ....
piranha ....
pygmy goat ....
python ....
stick insect ....
tarantula ....
amphibian ....
bird ....
fish ....
insect ....
mammal ....
reptile ....
spider ....

2 **Translate the words.**

Parts of the body

arm ....
beak ....
fin ....
finger ....
foot ....
hand ....
head ....
leg ....
neck ....
paw ....
tail ....
toe ....
wing ....

Vocabulary extension

3 **Match the photos to the words in the box. Use your dictionary if necessary. Write the words in English and in your language.**

| eagle | ladybug | ~~shark~~ | squirrel | turtle |

1 .....*shark*..... .... 2 ....

3 .... 4 ....

5 ....
....

Vocabulary

Unit vocabulary

1 Translate the words.

Activities

bowling ....

climbing ....

dancing ....

gymnastics ....

hiking ....

horseback riding

....

ice skating ....

kayaking ....

mountain biking

....

painting ....

playing an instrument

....

rollerblading ....

singing ....

surfing ....

2 Translate the words.

Seasons

spring ....

summer ....

autumn/fall ....

winter ....

Weather

cloudy ....

cold ....

foggy ....

hot ....

raining ....

snowing ....

sunny ....

warm ....

windy ....

Vocabulary extension

3 Match the photos to the words in the box. Use your dictionary if necessary. Write the words in English and in your language.

| flood | ice | lightning | rainbow | ~~storm~~ |

1 ....*storm*........ ....   2 ....

3 ....   4 ....

5 ....

....

Vocabulary

Delicious!

Unit vocabulary

1 Translate the words.

Food and drinks

banana ....

bread ....

broccoli ....

cheese ....

chicken ....

eggs ....

ham ....

juice ....

pasta ....

rice ....

salmon ....

sausage ....

shrimp ....

tea ....

tomatoes ....

tuna ....

water ....

yogurt ....

2 Translate the words.

Adjectives

clean ....

cold ....

delicious ....

dirty ....

disgusting ....

horrible ....

hot ....

large ....

noisy ....

quiet ....

small ....

wonderful ....

Vocabulary extension

3 Match the photos to the words in the box. Use your dictionary if necessary. Write the words in English and in your language.

carrots   cauliflower   cherries   ~~peaches~~   peas

1 ...*peaches*........ ....   2 ....

3 ....   4 ....

5 ....
   ....

Vocabulary

Modern History

Unit vocabulary

1 Translate the words.

Ordinal numbers and years

first ....

second ....

third ....

fourth ....

fifth ....

twentieth ....

twenty-second ....

thirty-first ....

nineteen twelve

....

nineteen twenty-two

....

nineteen forty-two

....

two thousand

....

two thousand four

....

two thousand eleven

....

2 Translate the words.

Regular verbs

answer ....

ask ....

call ....

close ....

invent ....

like ....

listen ....

stop ....

study ....

talk ....

travel ....

work ....

Vocabulary extension

3 Match the photos to the words in the box. Use your dictionary if necessary. Write the words in English and in your language.

| cook do the dishes help open sweep |

1 ......*cook*...... ....   2 ....

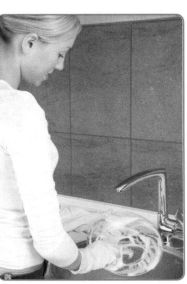 

3 ....   4 ....

5 ....

....

Vocabulary

Travel

Unit vocabulary

1 Translate the words.

Means of transportation

bike ....
boat ....
bus ....
canoe ....
car ....
helicopter ....
motorcycle ....
plane ....
scooter ....
subway ....
train ....
truck ....
van ....
drive ....
fly ....
ride ....
sail ....
take ....

2 Translate the words.

Clothes

boots ....
coat ....
dress ....
hat ....
jeans ....
pajamas ....
pants ....
sandals ....
scarf ....
shorts ....
skirt ....
sneakers ....
sweater ....

Vocabulary extension

3 Match the photos to the words in the box. Use your dictionary if necessary. Write the words in English and in your language.

| ~~belt~~ | gloves | jacket | slippers | socks |

1 ......*belt*........ ....

2 ....

3 ....

4 ....

5 ....
....

Vocabulary

Technology Time

Unit vocabulary

1 Translate the words.

Technology

blog ....

broadband ....

digital radio ....

e-reader ....

flash drive ....

IM (instant messaging)

....

interactive whiteboard

....

netbook ....

screen ....

smart phone ....

social networking site

....

Wi-Fi ....

2 Translate the phrases.

Technology phrases

charge your cell phone

....

chat online ....

download movies

....

download music

....

download videos

....

go online ....

send an email ....

send a text ....

use a search engine

....

use the Internet ....

use Wi-Fi ....

write a blog ....

Vocabulary extension

3 Match the photos to the words in the box. Use your dictionary if necessary. Write the words in English and in your language.

| document | keyboard | ~~mouse~~ | mouse pad | printer |

1 ......_mouse_...... ....   2 ....

3 ....   4 ....

5 ....
....

Speaking and Listening

Talking about position

• Speaking

1 Look at the pictures and complete the conversations with these words. Then listen and check.

39

behind	in	in front of	next to
on	under	~~Where~~	

A ¹ *Where* are my watch and my wallet?
B They're ² .... the table. Your watch is ³ .... the phone.

A Do you have my magazines?
B No, I don't. They're ⁴ .... the box ⁵ .... your desk.

A Where's my cell phone?
B It's ⁶ .... the laptop.
A Where's the laptop?
B It's ⁷ .... you!

2 Complete the conversation with these words and phrases. Then listen and check.

40

desk	doesn't	front	in
isn't	next	where	~~Where's~~

Sister ¹ *Where's* my blue pen?
Brother I don't know. I don't have your pen. Is it on the ² .... ?
Sister No. It isn't on the desk, and it isn't ³ .... to the phone.
Brother Is it ⁴ .... your backpack?
Sister No, it ⁵ ....
Brother Does Mom have it?
Sister No, she ⁶ ....
Brother Look! There's your pen. It's in ⁷ .... of the TV.
Sister Great! Thanks. Now, do we have a notebook?
Brother Yes. I have a notebook, but I don't know ⁸ .... it is!

• Listening

3 Listen to the conversation between Joe and his mom. Mark Joe's things.

41

wallet ☐   backpack ☑   soccer ball ☐

magazines ☐   cell phone ☐   schoolbooks ☐

DVDs ☐   MP3 player ☐   soccer cleats ☐

4 Listen again. Read where things are and write the name.

41

1 It's behind the door.   *backpack*
2 They're on the desk.   ....
3 They're under the bed.   ....
4 It's next to the laptop.   ....
5 It's in Joe's backpack.   ....

Speaking and Listening

Orders and warnings

• Speaking

1 Look at the pictures and write the correct order
42 or warning. Then listen and check.

> | Be careful! | ~~Don't shout!~~ | Don't touch it! |
> | Stop! | Wait for me! | Watch me! |

1 *Don't shout!* 2 .... 3 ....

4 .... 5 .... 6 ....

2 Complete the conversation with these words.
43 Then listen and check.

> | Call | do | don't | enjoy |
> | Go | Have | Let's | ~~party~~ |

Mom Jack, are you ready to go to Ana's ¹ *party*?
Jack Yes, Mom.
Mom OK. ² .... and get in the car,
please. And ³ .... forget
the present for Ana.
Jack Where is it?
Mom It's on the table in the kitchen.
Jack ⁴ .... go.

Mom We're here. Do you have your cell phone?
Jack Yes.
Mom Good. ⁵ .... me at the end of
the party. I can come and pick you up.
Jack OK.
Mom ⁶ .... fun and ⁷ ....
the party.
Jack Thanks, Mom. Bye.
Mom Don't ⁸ .... anything silly!

• Listening

3 Listen to the teacher and students on a school
44 trip. Circle the correct word or phrase.

1 Don't run or *shout* / *climb* on the statues.
2 Don't touch the *animals* / *objects*.
3 Stay with your *teacher* / *group*.
4 Don't go *outside* / *into the café*.
5 Come back here at *twelve o'clock* /
twelve thirty.
6 Look at those *boots* / *toys*.

4 Listen again. Are the statements true (T)
44 or false (F)?

1 The students are in a museum.   *T*
2 They have two hours to look around.
3 The boots are very small.
4 There's an old table.
5 There's a dinosaur behind Louise.

Speaking and Listening

Time

• Speaking

1 Complete the conversations with the correct
45 times. Then listen and check.

1

A What time is it, please?

B ⏰ It's *ten thirty-five*.

2

A When does the soccer game start?

B ⏰ It starts at ....

3

A What time does the party end?

B ⏰ It ends at ....

4

A It's ⏰ ....

B We're early. Class doesn't start until

⏰ ....

2 Read the conversation and choose the correct
46 words. Then listen and check.

Fred Jack Lemming's in the bookstore this
¹ *afternoon* / *today* with his new book.
He's there from two ² *o'clock* / *starts*
until half ³ *to* / *past* three.

Emily Really? He's a great actor.

Sylvia ⁴ *I don't know* / *I know*. I love him.

Fred Do you want to come to the store
with us and see him?

Emily Of course I do. ⁵ *What* / *When* time
is the bus?

Sylvia It leaves at ⁶ *twelve* / *time* ten.

Emily What ⁷ *time* / *o'clock* is it now?

Fred It's ⁸ *finishes* / *half* past eleven.

Sylvia Let's walk to the bus stop.

Emily I'm so excited!

• Listening

3 Listen to the conversation. Mark the correct clocks.
47

1 Maria's lesson starts at ☑ ☐

2 It ends at ☐ ☐

3 The movie starts at ☐ ☐

4 It ends at ☐ ☐

5 The time is now ☐ ☐

6 They meet at ☐ ☐

4 Listen again. Answer the questions.
47
1 Is the movie on TV?   *No, it isn't.*

2 Is the movie about aliens?

....

3 Does Maria have a music lesson?

....

4 How long is Maria's lesson?

....

5 Does Maria want to see the movie?

....

Speaking and Listening

Likes and dislikes

• Speaking

1 **Cross out the incorrect sentences. Then listen**
48 **and repeat.**

1 a ~~I not like doing puzzles.~~
  b I don't like doing puzzles.
2 a We love listening to pop music.
  b We love listen to pop music.
3 a Does he like cooking?
  b Likes he cooking?
4 a Karen is hating getting up early.
  b Karen hates getting up early.
5 a My mom and dad does like going
    to restaurants.
  b My mom and dad like going to restaurants.

2 **Complete the conversation with these words**
49 **and phrases. Then listen and check.**

tank

Do	don't	hate	likes
~~love~~	I	other dogs	watching

Carrie I'm so excited! We have a new cat.
I ¹ *love* playing with her. ² ....
you like animals? Do you have a pet?

James Yes. We have some fish. I like
³ .... them, but I
⁴ .... cleaning the fish tank.

Amy We have a dog named Daisy.
⁵ .... like taking her for a walk,
but she likes chasing ⁶ .... ,
and she sometimes runs away. She
⁷ .... jumping into the river too,
and she often sprays water on me.
I ⁸ .... like getting wet.

Carrie I'm glad we have a cat! She's easy
to take care of.

• Listening

3 **Listen to the conversation. Are the statements**
50 **true (T) or false (F)?**

1 *The X Factor* is on TV tonight.   *T*
2 Monica and George like watching *The X Factor*.
3 George likes watching sports on TV.
4 George is a Real Madrid fan.
5 George's favorite show is about sports.

4 **Listen again. Answer the questions.**
50 1 Why is Monica happy?
   Because The X Factor *is her favorite show.*
2 Why doesn't George like *The X Factor*?
   ....
   ....
3 Does Monica like watching soccer?
   ....
   ....
4 What's George's favorite show?
   ....
   ....
5 What does George like learning about?
   ....
   ....

Speaking and Listening

Expressing surprise

• Speaking

1 Match the statements (1–5) to the responses
51 (a–e). Then listen and check.

wild deer

1 This is a beautiful place. It's very quiet.   e
2 The mail carrier's here. There's a letter for you.
3 That store sells cheap posters.
4 I got Taylor Swift's autograph!
5 We have tickets for *American Idol*!

a Oh really? Great! I want a new poster
  for my room.
b Wow! How cool! When is it?
c Really? Who's it from?
d How amazing! Can you get it for me, too?
e Look! There are some deer over there.

2 Read the conversation and choose the
52 correct options. Then listen and check.

Dad	¹ We're here! / *See you later.*
Harry	Are we staying in this room?
Dad	Yes, we are.
Harry	² *Yuck!* / *Wow!* It's awesome. The beds are big.
Lizzie	And there's a computer and a TV.
Harry	We can see the town square from our window.
Lizzie	³ *I don't know.* / *Look!* There's a purple statue.
Harry	That isn't a real ⁴ *statue* / *purple.* It's a man on a box!
Lizzie	⁵ *Really?* / *Amazing?* It looks real.
Harry	I know. It's so ⁶ *cool* / *favorite.*
Lizzie	Dad, can we go and take a photo of him?
Dad	OK, but come back quickly.

• Listening

3 Listen to the conversation. Are the statements
53 true (T) or false (F)?

1 Brenda is Richard's aunt.   *T*
2 Her visit is a surprise.
3 She gives Richard a bike.
4 She stays for dinner.
5 Richard goes to the studio with Brenda.

4 Listen again. Answer the questions.
53
1 Who does Richard tell that Brenda's here?
  He tells his mom and dad.
2 Why does Brenda give Richard a present?
....
3 What does Brenda give him?
....
4 When is Brenda's interview?
....
5 Where is the interview?
....

Speaking and Listening

Ordering food

● Speaking

1 Match the questions (1–5) to the answers (a–e).
54 Then listen and check.

1 Can we sit here, please?   *d*
2 Are you ready to order?
3 Would you like some garlic bread?
4 Would you like anything to drink?
5 How is your food?

a No, thank you.
b It's delicious.
c Yes, we are.
d Yes, of course. Here's the menu.
e Yes. I'd like a glass of water, please.

2 Complete the conversation with these words.
55 Then listen and check.

anything	glass	I'll	like
OK	ready	~~table~~	Would

Boy   Let's sit at this ¹ *table*.
Dad   Yes. It's better than the table next to the door.
Waiter Are you ² .... to order?
Boy   I am. I'd like an egg sandwich and a strawberry smoothie, please.
Dad   And ³ .... have a chicken sandwich with mayonnaise, please.
Waiter Would you like ⁴ .... to drink?
Dad   Can I have a ⁵ .... of orange juice, please?
Waiter Yes, of course. ⁶ .... you like some chips with your sandwiches?
Dad   No. I'm ⁷ .... , thanks.
Boy   I'd ⁸ .... some chips, please.

● Listening

3 Listen to the conversation. Choose
56 the correct options.

1 They sit next to the *door* / (window.)
2 The waiter gives them *some water* / *the menus*.
3 Olivia would like *pasta* / *chicken* with tomato sauce.
4 Two people drink *orange* / *apple* juice.
5 They are in a *restaurant* / *café*.

4 Listen again. Complete the order.
56

Food	Drinks
• Customer 1	
.... with tomato sauce	orange juice
• Customer 2	
.... and broccoli	....
• Customer 3	
ham and cheese	apple juice

Speaking and Listening

Talking about the past

• Speaking

1 Complete the sentences with these time words
57 and phrases. Then listen and check.

| minutes ago | morning | ~~night~~ |
| seven years | the 1970s | yesterday |

1 **A** Where were they last *night*?
  B They were at home.
2 **A** Was there any homework .... ?
  B No, there wasn't.
3 He was late to school this ....
4 The teacher was in the classroom
  five ....
5 I like clothes from ....
6 He went to that school for ....

2 Complete the conversation with these words
58 and phrases. Then listen and check.

| ago | didn't | ~~for~~ | last |
| twenty | yesterday | 1980s | |

Dad   Look! That's our old house. We lived
        there ¹ *for* five years.
Clara I don't remember it.
Dad   You ² .... live there. I lived
        there in the ³ .... when I was
        a child.
Clara I didn't know you were from Atlanta.
Dad   Yes, Grandma and Grandpa moved to
        San Diego about ⁴ .... years
        ⁵ ....
Clara I like their new house. Can we visit them
        this weekend?
Dad   Sure. Grandma called me ⁶ ....
        Grandpa painted the living room orange
        ⁷ .... week. I want to see it!
Clara Me too! It sounds amazing!

• Listening

3 Listen to the conversation. Are the statements
59 true (T) or false (F)?

1 Donna Martin is an actor.   T
2 She arrived in Canada last month.   .....
3 This is her first visit.   .....
4 Her new movie is called *Generation Rox*.   .....
5 The movie is about three girls.   .....
6 Donna thinks the movie is very funny.   .....

4 Listen again. Answer the questions.
59
1 Where does Donna come from?
  She's from the US.
2 When was she in Canada?
  ....
3 When were the girls in the movie in New York?
  ....
4 How long were the girls in New York?
  ....
5 What music does Donna like?
  ....

Talking on the phone

• Speaking

1 Complete the conversations with the correct phrase. Then listen and check.
60

> Is Justin there, please? Just a minute.
> ~~This is her mom.~~ Who's this?

1

Bonnie's mom	Hello.
Ira	Hello. Is this Bonnie?
Bonnie's mom	No, it isn't. *This is her mom.*

2

Denzil	Hello.
Natalie	Hello. Is Frank there?
Denzil	Yes, he is. ....
Natalie	It's Natalie.

3

Cathy	Hello. This is Cathy.
Justin's dad	Hi, Cathy.
Cathy	....
Justin's dad	No, I'm sorry. Justin isn't here at the moment.

4

Charlie	Hello. This is Charlie. Can I speak to Anita, please?
Cameron	.... – Anita, Charlie's on the phone for you!

2 Read the conversation and choose the correct options. Then listen and check.
61

Brad's dad	Hello.
Connie	¹ *Hold on /* Hello, is this Brad?
Brad's dad	No, it isn't. ² *This is / I am* his dad.
Connie	Oh. Hi, Mr. Jones. Can I ³ *speak / have* to Brad, please?
Brad's dad	Yes, of course. ⁴ *See / Here* he is.
Connie	Hi, Brad. It's me, Connie.
Brad	Hello, Connie. How are you?
Connie	I'm fine, ⁵ *please / thanks*. Do you have Jordan's cell phone number?
Brad	Yes, ⁶ *only / just* a minute. It's 377 950-3729.
Connie	That's great. Thanks very much. Bye!
Brad	See you ⁷ *later / minute*.

• Listening

3 Listen to the telephone conversation. These sentences are useful for talking on the phone. Mark the sentences you hear.
62

1 Joel here. ☐
  Joel speaking. ☑
2 Can I speak to Eve, please? ☐
  Is Eve there, please? ☐
3 Who's speaking, please? ☐
  Who is it, please? ☐
4 Just a minute. ☐
  Hold on. ☐
5 Can you speak up, please? ☐
  Can you talk louder, please? ☐

4 Listen again. Answer the questions.
62

1 What club does Rob ask about?
  He asks about the Wildlife Club.
2 Did Eve go to the club yesterday?
  ....
3 Where is the trip to?
  ....
4 What date is the trip?
  ....
5 Can Rob go on the trip?
  ....

Speaking and Listening

Asking for information

• Speaking

1 Match the questions (1–5) to the answers (a–e).
63 Then listen and check.

1 What happened last night?   *d*
2 What are you going to do?
3 I downloaded that new movie yesterday.
4 Can you tell us more about your blog?
5 What is she planning for next year?

a I'm going to send an email to the principal.
b Tell me about it.
c She's going to study computer science.
d I dropped my phone, and it doesn't work now.
e I write about our band and all our concerts.

2 Complete the conversation with these words.
64 Then listen and check.

bank	car	going	happened
more	~~newspaper~~	saw	Tell

Will Wow! Look at this ¹ *newspaper* article. It's about a bank robbery here in Buffalo.
Ross Oh, yes!
Will Well, I ² .... the robbers.
Ross Really? ³ .... me about it.
Will Last Saturday morning I was downtown, outside the ⁴ .... Suddenly two men got out of a ⁵ ....
Ross What ⁶ .... next? Tell me ⁷ ....
Will They ran into the bank. I'm sure they were the robbers. I saw them very clearly.
Ross What are you ⁸ .... to do?
Will I'm going to tell the police what I saw.

• Listening

3 Listen to the conversation. Are the statements
65 true (T) or false (F)?

1 Simon fell off his bike.   *T*
2 A boy ran in front of the bike.   .....
3 The dog was hurt.   .....
4 Simon is going to ride his bike
   in the park after dinner.   .....
5 There's a good movie on TV in the evening. .....

4 Listen again. Answer the questions.
65 1 Where were Paul and Simon?
   They were in the park.
2 Was it Paul's dog?
   ....
3 Did Simon hit the dog?
   ....
4 Is Simon's leg clean?
   ....
5 What is Simon going to do this evening?
   ....

Pronunciation

Consonants

Symbol	Example	Your examples
/p/	**p**ark	
/b/	**b**ig	
/t/	**t**alk	
/d/	**d**og	
/k/	**c**ar	
/g/	**g**ood	
/tʃ/	**ch**air	
/dʒ/	**j**ump	
/f/	**f**ly	
/v/	**v**ideo	
/θ/	**th**ree	
/ð/	**th**ey	
/s/	**s**wim	
/z/	**z**oo	
/ʃ/	**sh**op	
/ʒ/	televi**si**on	
/h/	**h**ot	
/m/	**m**eet	
/n/	**n**ew	
/ŋ/	si**ng**	
/l/	**l**aptop	
/r/	**r**oom	
/j/	**y**ellow	
/w/	**w**atch	

Vowels

Symbol	Example	Your examples
/ɪ/	**i**nsect	
/ɛ/	l**e**g	
/æ/	h**a**m	
/ɑ/	b**o**x	
/ʌ/	f**u**n	
/ʊ/	p**u**t	
/i/	**ea**t	
/eɪ/	s**ai**l	
/aɪ/	m**y**	
/ɔɪ/	b**oy**	
/u/	b**oo**t	
/oʊ/	ph**o**ne	
/aʊ/	n**ow**	
/ɪr/	h**ear**	
/ɛr/	h**air**	
/ɑr/	**ar**m	
/ɔ/	d**o**g	
/ʊr/	t**our**	
/ɔr/	d**oor**	
/ə/	**a**mong	
/ɚ/	sh**ir**t	

Pronunciation practice

Unit 1 • Short forms

1 Listen and repeat.

66
1 I do not have   I don't have
2 He does not have   He doesn't have
3 They do not have   They don't have
4 She does not have   She doesn't have

2 Listen. Mark the sentence you hear.

67
1 a We do not have the camera. ☐
  b We don't have the camera. ☐
2 a The dog does not have the ball. ☐
  b The dog doesn't have the ball. ☐
3 a You do not have your wallet. ☐
  b You don't have your wallet. ☐
4 a He does not have a watch. ☐
  b He doesn't have a watch. ☐

3 Listen and repeat.

68
1 She doesn't have a ruler.
2 I don't have an eraser.
3 He doesn't have a pen.
4 You don't have a game console.

Unit 2 • Silent letters

1 Listen and repeat.

69
1 The snake can't walk, but it can swim.
2 I know your sister.
3 Talk to the man in the bank.
4 It can run and climb trees.
5 The guitar's on the table.

2 Which words from Exercise 1 have a silent letter? Write the words.

1 ....
2 ....
3 ....
4 ....
5 ....

3 Listen and check.
70

Unit 3 • -s endings

1 Listen and repeat.

71
1 like<u>s</u>   /s/   She like<u>s</u> me.
2 play<u>s</u>   /z/   He play<u>s</u> in the backyard.
3 watch<u>es</u>   /ɪz/   The cat watch<u>es</u> the birds.

2 Listen and complete the table with these verbs.

72

dances	flies	jumps
runs	walks	washes

/s/	/z/	/ɪz/
....	....	....
....	....	....

3 Listen and check.
73

Unit 4 • Contrastive stress

1 Listen and repeat.

74
1 **A** I can't swim.
  B No, but you can skate. I can't.
2 **A** Jess likes playing soccer.
  B Really? I don't. I like playing basketball.
3 Peter likes watching movies. But Derek likes playing computer games.
4 I have a new watch.
5 **A** There's a cat in the backyard.
  B No, there isn't. That's our dog!

2 Listen again. Circle the stressed words in Exercise 1.
74

3 Listen and check.
75

Unit 5 • -ing endings

1 Listen and repeat.

76
1 eat   eating   3 climb   climbing
2 dance   dancing

2 Listen. Circle the word you hear.

77
1 skate   skating   4 sing   singing
2 rainy   raining   5 clean   cleaning
3 study   studying   6 start   starting

3 Listen and repeat.

78
1 He's going to school.
2 We're running.
3 She's having lunch.
4 They're swimming.
5 I'm playing a computer game.

Unit 6 • Word stress

1 Listen and repeat.

79

• •	• • •
chicken	po<u>ta</u>to

2 Listen and choose the word with the correct stress.

80
1 • • <u>yo</u>gurt   • • yo<u>gurt</u>
2 • • <u>ca</u>rrot   • • ca<u>rrot</u>
3 • • • bro<u>cco</u>li   • • • <u>bro</u>ccoli
4 • • <u>dai</u>ry   • • dai<u>ry</u>
5 • • <u>wa</u>ter   • • wa<u>ter</u>
6 • • • <u>to</u>mato   • • • to<u>ma</u>to
7 • • <u>tu</u>na   • • tu<u>na</u>
8 • • • <u>ba</u>nana   • • • ba<u>na</u>na
9 • • <u>sal</u>mon   • • sal<u>mon</u>
10 • • pa<u>sta</u>   • • <u>pa</u>sta

3 Listen and check.

81

Unit 7 • -ed endings

1 Listen and repeat.

82
1 listened   /d/   We <u>listened</u> to the teacher.
2 invented   /ɪd/   He <u>invented</u> the radio.
3 talked   /t/   She <u>talked</u> to her friend.

2 Listen and complete the table with these words.

83

called	liked	opened
started	wanted	watched

/d/	/ɪd/	/t/
....	....	....
....	....	....

3 Listen and check.

84

Unit 8 • Sounding polite

1 Listen to two versions of the same phone conversation. Which sounds more polite?

85

Debbie's sister	Hello.
Jake	Hi. This is Jake. Is this Debbie?
Debbie's sister	No, it's her sister. Do you want to talk to her?
Jake	Yes. Is she there?
Debbie's sister	Yes, she is. Just a minute.

2 Listen. Decide which pronunciation is polite (P) and which is not polite (NP).

86
1 a Can I speak to Dave, please?
  b Can I speak to Dave, please?
2 a Who's speaking, please?
  b Who's speaking, please?
3 a This is Liam's dad.
  b This is Liam's dad.

3 Listen and repeat.

87

Unit 9 • Weak form of to

1 Listen and repeat.

88
1 It's going to snow.
2 They aren't going to go on vacation.
3 Is he going to buy the DVD?

2 Listen and mark the sentences with the weak form of to.

89
1 ☐   3 ☐   5 ☐
2 ☐   4 ☐   6 ☐

3 Listen and check.

90

Irregular Verb List

Verb	Past Simple	Past Particple
be	was/were	been
become	became	become
begin	began	begun
break	broke	broken
bring	brought	brought
build	built	built
buy	bought	bought
can	could	been able
catch	caught	caught
choose	chose	chosen
come	came	come
cost	cost	cost
cut	cut	cut
do	did	done
drink	drank	drunk
drive	drove	driven
eat	ate	eaten
feel	felt	felt
fight	fought	fought
find	found	found
fly	flew	flown
forget	forgot	forgotten
get	got	gotten
give	gave	given
go	went	gone/been
have	had	had
hear	heard	heard
hold	held	held
keep	kept	kept

Verb	Past Simple	Past Particple
know	knew	known
leave	left	left
lose	lost	lost
make	made	made
mean	meant	meant
meet	met	met
pay	paid	paid
put	put	put
read /rid/	read /rɛd/	read /rɛd/
run	ran	run
say	said	said
see	saw	seen
sell	sold	sold
send	sent	sent
sing	sang	sung
sit	sat	sat
sleep	slept	slept
speak	spoke	spoken
swim	swam	swum
take	took	taken
teach	taught	taught
tell	told	told
think	thought	thought
throw	threw	thrown
understand	understood	understood
wake	woke	woken
wear	wore	worn
win	won	won
write	wrote	written

My Assessment Profile   Starter Unit

1 What can I do? Mark (✓) the options in the table.

⏪ = I need to study this again.   ⏸ = I'm not sure about this.   ▶ = I'm happy with this.   ⏩ = I do this very well.

		⏪	⏸	▶	⏩
Vocabulary (Student's Book pages 4 and 5)	• I can talk about countries and nationalities. • I can use numbers 1 to 100. • I can use the alphabet to spell words. • I can talk about classroom objects. • I can talk about the days of the week and the months of the year. • I can understand classroom language.				
Grammar (SB pages 6 and 7)	• I can use all forms of *to be* in the Present simple. • I can use *Wh* question words. • I can use *this, that, these* and *those*.				
Reading (SB page 8)	• I can understand a pamphlet about a wildlife club.				
Listening (SB page 9)	• I can understand people talking about themselves.				
Speaking (SB page 9)	• I can ask for information.				
Writing (SB page 9)	• I can complete a form.				

2 What new words and expressions can I remember?

words ....

expressions ....

3 How can I practice other new words and expressions?

record them on my MP3 player ☐   write them in a notebook ☐

practice them with a friend ☐   translate them into my language ☐

4 What English have I learned outside class?

	words	expressions
on the radio		
in songs		
in movies		
on the Internet		
on TV		
with friends		

My Assessment Profile   Unit

1 What can I do? Mark (✓) the options in the table.

⏪ = I need to study this again.   ⏸ = I'm not sure about this.   ▶ = I'm happy with this.   ⏩ = I do this very well.

		⏪	⏸	▶	⏩
Vocabulary (Student's Book pages 10 and 13)	• I can talk about my belongings. • I can use contrasting adjectives to describe things.				
Reading (SB pages 11 and 16)	• I can read and understand a magazine feature about people's collections and an interview from a magazine problem page.				
Grammar (SB pages 12 and 15)	• I can use *have* to talk about possession. • I can use possessive adjectives and possessive *'s*.				
Pronunciation (SB page 12)	• I can pronounce the short forms of *do not*.				
Speaking (SB pages 14 and 15)	• I can use prepositions of place to talk about where things are.				
Listening (SB page 16)	• I can understand an interviewer talking to different people about collections.				
Writing (SB page 17)	• I can use capital letters, periods and apostrophes. • I can write a personal profile.				

2 What new words and expressions can I remember?

words ....

expressions ....

3 How can I practice other new words and expressions?

record them on my MP3 player ☐   write them in a notebook ☐

practice them with a friend ☐   translate them into my language ☐

4 What English have I learned outside class?

	words	expressions
on the radio		
in songs		
in movies		
on the Internet		
on TV		
with friends		

My Assessment Profile Unit

1 **What can I do? Mark (✓) the options in the table.**

⏪ = I need to study this again. ⏸ = I'm not sure about this. ▶ = I'm happy with this. ⏩ = I do this very well.

		⏪	⏸	▶	⏩
Vocabulary (Student's Book pages 20 and 23)	• I can talk about places in a town. • I can use action verbs.				
Reading (SB pages 21 and 26)	• I can understand an advertisement for computer games and read descriptions of two New York parks on a website.				
Grammar (SB pages 22 and 25)	• I can use *there is/there are* with *some* and *any*. • I can talk about what I and other people can and can't do.				
Pronunciation (SB page 23)	• I can pronounce words with silent letters.				
Speaking (SB pages 24 and 25)	• I can give orders and warn people about danger.				
Listening (SB page 26)	• I can understand an audition for a part in a show.				
Writing (SB page 27)	• I can use the linking words *and, or* and *but*. • I can write a description of a town.				

2 **What new words and expressions can I remember?**

words ....

expressions ....

3 **How can I practice other new words and expressions?**

record them on my MP3 player ☐   write them in a notebook ☐

practice them with a friend ☐   translate them into my language ☐

4 **What English have I learned outside class?**

	words	expressions
on the radio		
in songs		
in movies		
on the Internet		
on TV		
with friends		

My Assessment Profile Unit

1 What can I do? Mark (✓) the options in the table.

⏪ = I need to study this again.   ⏸ = I'm not sure about this.   ▶ = I'm happy with this.   ⏩ = I do this very well.

		⏪	⏸	▶	⏩
Vocabulary (Student's Book pages 30 and 33)	• I can talk about my daily routine. • I can discuss the subjects I study at school.				
Reading (SB pages 31 and 36)	• I can read a blog about a big family, and I can understand and complete a quiz about schools in other countries.				
Grammar (SB pages 32 and 35)	• I can use the Present simple to talk about routines. • I can use the Present simple to ask other people about their routines.				
Pronunciation (SB page 32)	• I can hear the difference between the Present simple endings /s/, /z/ and /ɪz/.				
Speaking (SB pages 34 and 35)	• I can ask and answer questions about time.				
Listening (SB page 36)	• I can understand a radio interview about a school day in China.				
Writing (SB page 37)	• I can use time phrases with *on*, *in* and *at*. • I can write an email about a school day.				

2 What new words and expressions can I remember?

words ....

expressions ....

3 How can I practice other new words and expressions?

record them on my MP3 player ☐   write them in a notebook ☐

practice them with a friend ☐   translate them into my language ☐

4 What English have I learned outside class?

	words	expressions
on the radio		
in songs		
in movies		
on the Internet		
on TV		
with friends		

My Assessment Profile   Unit

1 **What can I do? Mark (✓) the options in the table.**

⏪ = I need to study this again.   ⏸ = I'm not sure about this.   ▶ = I'm happy with this.   ⏩ = I do this very well.

		⏪	⏸	▶	⏩
Vocabulary (Student's Book pages 44 and 47)	• I can talk about unusual animals and animal categories. • I can talk about parts of the body to describe animals and people.				
Reading (SB pages 45 and 50)	• I can read and understand an online interview with a zookeeper about his work. • I can read a magazine article about unusual pets.				
Grammar (SB pages 46 and 49)	• I can use adverbs of frequency. • I can ask *Wh* questions using the Present simple. • I can talk about rules using *must* and *mustn't*.				
Pronunciation (SB page 49)	• I can identify which words are stressed in sentences.				
Speaking (SB pages 48 and 49)	• I can express my likes and dislikes.				
Listening (SB page 50)	• I can understand a radio interview about a special animal.				
Writing (SB page 51)	• I can write a fact sheet about an unusual animal.				

2 **What new words and expressions can I remember?**

words   ....

expressions   ....

3 **How can I practice other new words and expressions?**

record them on my MP3 player   ☐   write them in a notebook   ☐

practice them with a friend   ☐   translate them into my language   ☐

4 **What English have I learned outside class?**

	words	expressions
on the radio		
in songs		
in movies		
on the Internet		
on TV		
with friends		

My Assessment Profile Unit

1 **What can I do? Mark (✓) the options in the table.**

⏪ = I need to study this again.　⏸ = I'm not sure about this.　▶ = I'm happy with this.　⏩ = I do this very well.

		⏪	⏸	▶	⏩
Vocabulary (Student's Book pages 54 and 57)	• I can describe different freetime activities. • I can talk about the weather and the seasons.				
Reading (SB pages 55 and 60)	• I can read a magazine article about a stuntman's day and understand some poems about the weather.				
Grammar (SB pages 56 and 59)	• I can use the Present continuous to talk about things that are happening now. • I can decide when to use the Present continuous and when to use the Present simple.				
Pronunciation (SB page 56)	• I can pronounce the Present continuous ending -ing.				
Speaking (SB pages 58 and 59)	• I can express surprise in different situations.				
Listening (SB page 60)	• I can understand people describing their preferences.				
Writing (SB page 61)	• I can write a blog entry about an exchange trip.				

2 **What new words and expressions can I remember?**

words ....

expressions ....

3 **How can I practice other new words and expressions?**

record them on my MP3 player ☐　　　write them in a notebook ☐

practice them with a friend ☐　　　translate them into my language ☐

4 **What English have I learned outside class?**

	words	expressions
on the radio		
in songs		
in movies		
on the Internet		
on TV		
with friends		

My Assessment Profile Unit

1) **What can I do? Mark (✓) the options in the table.**

⏪ = I need to study this again.   ⏸ = I'm not sure about this.   ▶ = I'm happy with this.   ⏩ = I do this very well.

		⏪	⏸	▶	⏩
Vocabulary (Student's Book pages 64 and 67)	• I can talk about different types of food and drinks, and food categories. • I can use contrasting adjectives.				
Reading (SB pages 65 and 70)	• I can read a magazine article about food and understand a newspaper feature about special restaurants.				
Grammar (SB pages 66 and 69)	• I can use countable and uncountable nouns and *(how) many/ (how) much/a lot of*. • I can make comparisons using short or long adjectives.				
Pronunciation (SB page 66)	• I can hear the stress in different words for food and drinks.				
Speaking (SB pages 68 and 69)	• I can order food.				
Listening (SB page 70)	• I can understand people giving different information about national dishes.				
Writing (SB page 71)	• I can use the sequence words *first, then* and *finally*. • I can write instructions for a recipe.				

2) **What new words and expressions can I remember?**

words ....

expressions ....

3) **How can I practice other new words and expressions?**

record them on my MP3 player ☐   write them in a notebook ☐

practice them with a friend ☐   translate them into my language ☐

4) **What English have I learned outside class?**

	words	expressions
on the radio		
in songs		
in movies		
on the Internet		
on TV		
with friends		

My Assessment Profile   Unit

1 **What can I do? Mark (✓) the options in the table.**

⏮ = I need to study this again.   ⏸ = I'm not sure about this.   ▶ = I'm happy with this.   ⏭ = I do this very well.

		⏮	⏸	▶	⏭
Vocabulary (Student's Book pages 78 and 81)	• I can use and talk about ordinal numbers, years and dates. • I can use regular verbs.				
Reading (SB pages 79 and 84)	• I can read the text of a school project about the 1960s and understand a brochure for a museum exhibition about modern culture.				
Grammar (SB pages 80 and 83)	• I can use the Past simple of *to be* and *there was/there were*. • I can make statements using Past simple regular verbs.				
Pronunciation (SB page 81)	• I can hear the difference between the Past simple *-ed* endings /d/, /t/ and /ɪd/.				
Speaking (SB pages 82 and 83)	• I can use expressions to talk about the past.				
Listening (SB page 84)	• I can understand people describing what they do in a museum.				
Writing (SB page 85)	• I can use periods, commas, question marks and exclamation points. • I can write an essay about childhood.				

2 **What new words and expressions can I remember?**

words ....

expressions ....

3 **How can I practice other new words and expressions?**

record them on my MP3 player ☐   write them in a notebook ☐

practice them with a friend ☐   translate them into my language ☐

4 **What English have I learned outside class?**

	words	expressions
on the radio		
in songs		
in movies		
on the Internet		
on TV		
with friends		

My Assessment Profile Unit

1 **What can I do? Mark (✓) the options in the table.**

⏪ = I need to study this again.   ⏸ = I'm not sure about this.   ▶ = I'm happy with this.   ⏩ = I do this very well.

		⏪	⏸	▶	⏩
Vocabulary (Student's Book pages 88 and 91)	• I can talk about different means of transportation and use transportation verbs. • I can talk about clothes.				
Reading (SB pages 89 and 94)	• I can read an extract from a novel about a journey around the world and understand information from a textbook about a boy living in West Africa.				
Grammar (SB pages 90 and 93)	• I can make statements using Past simple irregular verbs. • I can ask questions using the Past simple.				
Pronunciation (SB page 93)	• I can sound polite.				
Speaking (SB pages 92 and 93)	• I can use the correct phrases for talking on the phone.				
Listening (SB page 94)	• I can understand an informal conversation.				
Writing (SB page 95)	• I can use paragraphs correctly in a text. • I can write a travel diary.				

2 **What new words and expressions can I remember?**

words ....

expressions ....

3 **How can I practice other new words and expressions?**

record them on my MP3 player ☐   write them in a notebook ☐

practice them with a friend ☐   translate them into my language ☐

4 **What English have I learned outside class?**

	words	expressions
on the radio		
in songs		
in movies		
on the Internet		
on TV		
with friends		

My Assessment Profile   Unit (9)

1. What can I do? Mark (✓) the options in the table.

⏮ = I need to study this again.   ⏸ = I'm not sure about this.   ▶ = I'm happy with this.   ⏭ = I do this very well.

		⏮	⏸	▶	⏭
Vocabulary (Student's Book pages 98 and 101)	• I can talk about different types of technology. • I can use technology phrases.				
Reading (SB pages 99 and 104)	• I can understand a magazine article about e-books and read chatroom entries about a technology-free week at school.				
Grammar (SB pages 100 and 103)	• I can use *be going to* to talk about future plans and intentions. • I can use the Present continuous to talk about future arrangements.				
Pronunciation (SB page 100)	• I can pronounce the weak form of *to* in *going to*.				
Speaking (SB pages 102 and 103)	• I can use phrases to ask for information.				
Listening (SB page 104)	• I can understand people talking about their plans.				
Writing (SB page 105)	• I can check my writing for mistakes. • I can write a story.				

2. What new words and expressions can I remember?

words ....

expressions ....

3. How can I practice other new words and expressions?

record them on my MP3 player ☐   write them in a notebook ☐

practice them with a friend ☐   translate them into my language ☐

4. What English have I learned outside class?

	words	expressions
on the radio		
in songs		
in movies		
on the Internet		
on TV		
with friends		

Pearson Education Limited
Edinburgh Gate
Harlow
Essex CM20 2JE
England
and Associated Companies throughout the world.

www.pearsonelt.com/moveit

© Pearson Education Limited 2015

Printed and bound in Poland by Zapolex
First published 2015, Ninth impression 2021
Set in 10.5/12.5pt LTC Helvetica Neue Light
ISBN: 978-1-4479-8271-5

Acknowledgements
We are grateful to the following for permission to reproduce copyright material:
Poetry on page 10 'Weather' from *101 Science Poems & Songs for Young Learners* by Meish Goldish. Scholastic Inc./Teaching Resources. Copyright © 1996 by Meish Goldish. Reprinted by permission.

Photo Acknowledgements
The publisher would like to thank the following for their kind permission to reproduce their photographs:

(Key: b-bottom; c-centre; l-left; r-right; t-top)

123RF.com: 114, Christian Delbert 17, Barbara Helgason 51tr, Dzianis Miraniuk 66tr; **Alamy Images:** Angela Hampton Picture Library 72l, Bill Bachman 30tl, Paul Carstairs 14cl, Ffotocymru 49, Jayfish 9tr, Gina Kelly 14r, Rafael Angel Irusta Machin 120tr, Bob Paroue-SC 74, Stock Foundry / Vibe Images 25br; **BananaStock:** 10tr; **Comstock Images:** 109tr; **Corbis:** Atlantide Phototravel / Massimo Borchi 117cl, Blend / Ned Frisk 35br, Comet / Randy Faris 101br, Corbis Outline / Beateworks / Scott Van Dyke 14cr, Corbis Outline / Steve Ellison 56, HO / Reuters 66tc, Image Source 6, Imagesource 47tr, Norgues-Orban / Sygma 60bl, Xinhua Press / Chen Kai 60tc; **Digital Vision:** Robert Harding World Imagery / Jim Reed 108tl; **DK Images:** Steve Teague 41; **Fotolia.com:** 126-135; **Getty Images:** Daniel Berehvlak 116tr, GP / Ivan Gavan 66tl, Dave Hogan 46cr, OJO Images / Robert Daly 119tr, Retrofile RF / George Marks 61cr, Alberto E. Rodriguez 46c, Stockbyte 30tc, Stone / Chris Ryan 116r, VStockLLC 106cl, WireImage / Jim Spellman 46cl, WireImage / Rebecca Sapp 115l; **iStockphoto:** amriphoto 30cr; **MedioImages:** 73tr; **MIXA Co., Ltd:** 51br; **NASA:** 60cr; **National Archives and Records Administration (NARA):** 60tl; **Pearson Education Ltd:** Jon Barlow 118cr, Sophie Bluy 51bc, Gareth Boden 35bl, 91tr, Ikat Design / Ann Cromack 70br, Jules Selmes 4tr, 51bl, 61bl, 72r, 105tl, 119cl, Studio 8 48, Tudor Photography 35cr; **Penguin Books Ltd:** 9cr; **PhotoDisc:** Steve Cole 104tr, Jules Frazier 14l; **Reuters:** Vincent Kessler 69tr; **Rex Features:** Sipa Press 60br; **Science Photo Library Ltd:** Ria Novosti 60bc; **Shutterstock. com:** Aispix by Imagesource 47bc, Ozerov Alexander 108cl, Alexgul 112tl, Anetapics 121tr, Blend 47bl, Rich Carey 107cl, Adriano Castelli 105cr, cbpix 107tl, ChameleonsEye 35t, Coprid 104cr, Creatista 117tr, Cynoclub 116cr, Frantisek Czanner 107b, Deklofenak 110cl, Erashov 9cl, Dmitry Fisher 104cl, Floridastock 107tr, Gorin 105cl, Hfng 47tc, Holbox 47tl, IKO 77cl, Iofoto 40t, Eric Isselee 20r, Lobur Alexey Ivanovich 111tl, Jhaz Photography 108cr, Matt Jones 116c, Karkas 111crr, KKulikov 9br, Luso Images 104b, Lori B.K. Mann 108b, Maridav 47br, James R Martin 30c, Matka_Wariatka 106b, Jiri Miklo 110tl, Robert Milek 112cl, Monkey Business Images 105bc, 110tr, mrpuiii 104tl, R. Nagy 30cl, Olinchuk 111b, Pakhnyushcha 107cr, Narcis Parfenti 105tr, Olga Popova 111cl, pressureUA 77tl, PRILL Mediendesign und Fotografie 109b, Christina Richards 110b, Roberts.J 51cl, Robootb 106cr, ronfromyork 108tr, Sagir 111tr, Santia 109cl, Julia Sapil 35c, Shutswis 112tr, Sinelyov 116cl, Danny Smythe 106tr, Artur Synenko 112cr, Pal Teravagimov 117tl, Vadico 51cr, Vanillaechoes 51tl, Vilax 77c, Valentyn Volkov 109tl, 109cr, Wavebreakmedia Ltd 110cr, Karen Wunderman 115tr, Yurok 112b, Zakhardoff 9bl; **Stockdisc:** 20l; **Susie Prescott:** 106tl; **The Independent:** 69tl; **The Kobal Collection:** Universal 64bl, Walt Disney Pictures 9tl; **Zuma Press:** Los Angeles Daily News / Michael Owen Baker 69bl

Cover images: *Front:* **Alamy Images:** Design Pics Inc.

All other images © Pearson Education

Every effort has been made to trace the copyright holders and we apologise in advance for any unintentional omissions. We would be pleased to insert the appropriate acknowledgement in any subsequent edition of this publication.

Special thanks to the following for their help during location photography:
Ascape Studios; Herts Young Mariners Base; Lullingstone Country Park; Pets Corner; Soprano, Sevenoaks; St. Matthew Academy; The Stag Community Arts Centre.

Illustrated by: Paula Franco: page 4 (top left), page 5, page 6, page 10 (bottom right), page 16 (bottom), page 18 (top right), page 21 (top right), page 22, page 28 (top left), page 81 (left), page 84, page 87, page 97; Sonia Alins: page 4 (centre right), page 8, page 11, page 13 (bottom right), page 21 (top right), page 23 (right), page 26, page 27 (1-2 & 4-7), page 30, page 36, page 38 (right), page 42 (top), page 45, page 48 (bottom right 2-4), page 50, page 52, page 53, page 54, page 56 (bottom), page 68, page 71 (bottom), page 73, page 76 (centre 1 & 3-7), page 81; Esteban Gómez: page 7, page 55, page 56 (top), page 76 (top), page 79, page 82, page 101, page 103, page 113, page 114, page 121; José Luís Ágreda: page 12, page 13 (top right), page 15, page 19, page 20 (bottom right), page 21 (left), page 23 (left), page 24 (left), page 25, page 34, page 89, page 91, page 93, page 95; Nancy Ortega page 76 (centre 2); José Antonio Rubio: page 10 (bottom left), page 20 (centre left), page 32, page 33, page 37, page 38 (left), page 39, page 40 (right), page 42 (bottom), page 44, page 58, page 59, page 61, page 62, page 63, page 65, page 71 (top), page 78, page 85, page 99 (bottom); Marcela Gómez Ruenes (A Corazón Abierto) page 27 (3 & 8), page 42 (bottom a), page 43, page 48 (bottom right 1).